Your Future In The Modern Medium

Your Future In The Modern Medium

DAN BLUME

Published by
CONTINENTAL MEDIA COMPANY
Post Office Box 31256
Hartford, Connecticut 06103

First Edition

Printed in the United States of America

Library of Congress Catalog Card Number
83-71022

ISBN 0-912349-00-X

For my wife Joanne, son Jared, and daughter Meredith

Contents

Page

PREFACE   xi

Chapter

One   *Careers in Radio*   1
Radio—A Dynamic, Fascinating Industry—
"How Can I Get Into Radio?"—What This
Book Will Do For You

Two   *The Development of Commercial*   7
Radio
Radio—The Product of an International
Effort—How it Works—The History of
American Commercial Radio—The Regulation
of Radio

Three   *Characteristics of Commercial Radio*   21
Stations
Two Basic Types of Stations—AM and FM—
Classes of Stations—Locations and Shapes of
Stations—Names, Slogans, and Symbols by
Which Stations are Known

Four   *Radio Station Management and*   31
Organizational Structure
The Objectives of Management—The General
Manager - Qualities and Qualifications—The
Duties of the General Manager—Organizational
Structures of Radio Stations

Five   *Radio Audiences and Programming*   41
The Golden Age of Radio—Targeted Audiences
and Modern Programming—Audience
Research—Program Patterns and Formats

Six   *The Program Department*   55
Factors Shaping the Organization of the
Program Department—The Program
Director—The Program Director's Staff—
Music, News, Sports, Production, Promotion,
and Traffic

Seven   *Radio Performers*   67
         Images, Characters, and Personalities Through
         Voices and Words—Radio Performers and
         Broadcast Roles—Disc Jockeys—Morning
         Men—Staff Announcers—Personalities—
         Newscasters—Sportscasters—Talk Show
         Hosts—Specialists

Eight   *Radio Sales*   81
         Radio—The Advertising Media—The Sales
         Department—The General Sales Manager—
         Salespersons and Account Executives—National
         Sales Representatives—Network Sales

Nine   *Radio Engineering*   91
         Radio Station Operator Licenses and
         Regulation—The Engineering Department—
         The Chief Engineer—The Chief Engineer's Staff

Ten   *Network Radio*   105
         The Rise, Fall, and Rise of Network Radio—
         Modern Network Radio—The Miracle of
         Satellite Technology—Network Administration
         and Management

Eleven   *Making It In Radio*   113
         Straight Talk and Advice from 19 Professionals
         Working in Programming, Sales, Engineering,
         Management, and Broadcast Education—
         Breaking Into Radio

GLOSSARY OF TERMS COMMONLY USED IN   145
RADIO BROADCASTING

SELECTED BIBLIOGRAPHY   163

INDEX   167

Contributors

JERRY BISHOP, Freelance Announcer and Morning Man, KGIL Radio, San Fernando, California

BOB CAIN, Anchorman, Cable News Network

JOHN G. CHANIN, Vice President-Sports, Mutual Broadcasting System

DON CHEVRIER, Sportscaster, ABC Radio and Television Networks and The Toronto Blue Jays, The American League, Major League Baseball

BOB CRAIG, Program Director, WMGK(FM), Philadelphia

PETER S. CRAWFORD, Vice President and Station Manager, WHDH, Boston

DONA S. GOODMAN, Account Executive, WPLR(FM) and WSCR, New Haven

DON IMUS, Morning Man, WNBC Radio, New York

CHUCK KAITON, Play-By-Play Man, The Hartford Whalers, National Hockey League

DONNA RUSTIGIAN McCARTHY, On-air Personality, WKRI, West Warwick, Rhode Island

BYRON N. McCLANAHAN, Vice President and General Manager, WKND Radio, Hartford

CHARLIE PARKER, Program Director, WDRC AM/FM, Hartford

RON PELL, Vice President and General Sales Manager, WDRC AM/FM, Hartford

JIM PERRY, Chief Engineer, WKSS(FM), Hartford

WILLIAM F. RASMUSSEN, Vice President, Satellite Syndicated Systems, Inc. and Founder of ESPN Cable Network

DICK ROBINSON, Founder and President of The Connecticut School of Broadcasting, Farmington and Stratford, Connecticut

PAULA E. SCHNEIDER, Account Executive, WNBC Radio, New York

ELTON L. SPITZER, General Manager of WLIR(FM), Garden City, New York and principal owner of WLYF(FM), South Bristol (Rochester), New York

WALT WHEELER, Reporter, WCBS/NewsRadio 88, New York

Preface

This book is for anyone who is attracted to the field of radio broadcasting. If you wish to explore the many, exciting careers offered by radio, the book will serve as your key to a bright future in this dynamic medium. It is also a resource for beginning broadcasters, persons involved in advertising, and those who want to know more about radio for professional or personal understanding. Although some of the contents will be elementary to experienced professionals, much will also enlighten them.

Radio is much more than "music, news, and sports." It is a huge industry that touches the lives of millions daily. More than 95 percent of the people in the United States listen to the radio during each week. The average radio listener spends 22 hours per week listening to the radio, and 95 percent of all cars in the United States are equipped with radios.

To exist and grow, the industry depends upon the diversified skills and talents of thousands of men and women. Contrary to popular belief, one need not have a great voice to enjoy a stimulating and rewarding career in radio. All disc jockeys, sportscasters, and other performers rely on the efforts of management, programming, sales, and engineering personnel for support in their work. If you have the *talent, drive,* and *knowledge of the industry*, you can make it in radio. And this book provides you with that knowledge.

After reviewing radio's history, size, importance, and scientific basis, the book explores the commercial radio station, the industry's basic unit, by examining its departments and the skills needed to make them run. Throughout, the origins of the industry are discussed in order to place modern radio and its regulation by the Federal Communications Commission into perspective. The future of the industry, the wonders of satellite communications, and the rebirth of network radio are also considered. Nineteen radio professionals — disc jockeys, newscasters, sportscasters, salespersons, network executives, general managers, an engineer, program directors, and others — give you first hand advice about radio. They show you how to determine if a career in radio is for you, and, if so, what you should do to prepare yourself for it, to get into the field, and to advance within the industry. A comprehensive glossary of the language of American radio is also provided.

I wish to express my sincere appreciation to all who assisted me in the preparation of this book, but I personally assume all responsibility for everything that appears herein. I offer my gratitude to Susan R. Bonchi for her outstanding editorial assistance and to Diane S. Busque for her dedicated supervision of the manuscript. For their patience, assistance, and encouragement, I am particularly grateful to Zim Barstein, WLIR(FM); Bob Craig, WMGK(FM); Charlie Parker, WDRC (AM/FM); Dick Robinson, The Connecticut School of Broadcasting, Inc.; Roy R. Russo, Esq., Cohn and Marks; Elton L. Spitzer, WLIR(FM), and Walt Wheeler, WCBS/NewsRadio 88. I am indebted to Jerry Bishop, KGIL; Bob Cain, Cable News Network; John G. Chanin, Mutual Broadcasting System; Don Chevrier, ABC Radio and Television; Peter S. Crawford, WHDH; Dona S. Goodman, WPLR(FM)/WSCR; Don Imus, WNBC; Chuck Kaiton, The Hartford Whalers, NHL; A. Anthony Kelsey, Esq., Arbitron Ratings Company; Donna Rustigian McCarthy, WKRI; Byron N. McClanahan, WKND; Ron Pell, WDRC AM/FM; Jim Perry, WKSS(FM); William F. Rasmussen, Satellite Syndicated Systems, and Paula E. Schneider, WNBC, for their contributions.

I extend my warmest gratitude to the hundreds of other wonderful people in and around broadcasting for providing me with valuable data and advice and to my great friends for their interest and encouragement. Finally, to my wife, son, and daughter, who put up with my many moods, I give a very special thanks for being my staunchest supporters.

Dan Blume

October, 1983
West Hartford, Connecticut

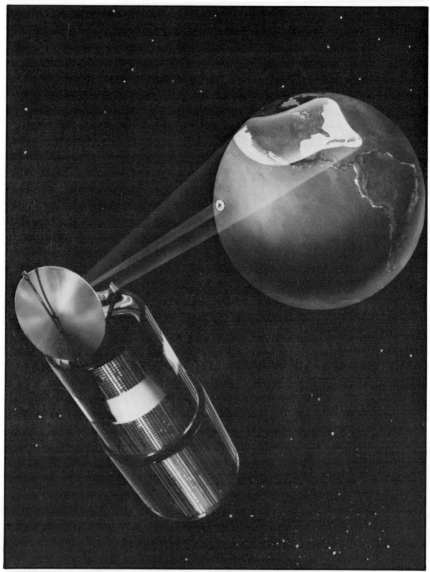

Westar V, a satellite launched on June 8, 1982, has a 24 transponder capacity and a design life of 10 years. It is located at 123 degrees West Longitude. *Courtesy of Western Union.*

Chapter One

Careers in Radio

Radio is a dynamic, fascinating industry that reaches, informs, and entertains over 225 million Americans each week. To exist, it depends on the talents, diversified skills, and dedication of thousands of people who operate more than 8,000 commercial stations, hundreds of public and educational stations, an increasing number of networks, and other businesses associated with the industry. To continue to grow and prosper, radio must have a constant supply of active, creative people whose imaginations and energy produce new ideas, develop fresh forms of broadcast service, and meet the competitive challenges of the industry.

The glamour and excitement of a career in radio attract many young people who dream of becoming disc jockeys, newscasters, and play-by-play announcers. Few outside the industry, however, understand that there is much more to radio than on-air personalities. Most are surprised by the wide range of professions and jobs radio encompasses. To appreciate the breadth of this range, one must comprehend the industry and the many different ways in which professionals function within it.

The commercial radio station is the basic unit of the industry. Other than the methods by which they are financed, professionally run public and educational stations function basically like commercial stations. In each phase of its construction and throughout its existence, a station depends on the efforts of numerous outside specialists. A new station gets its start when consulting engineers find a frequency for use at a particular geographical location that will not interfere with existing stations using the same or adjacent frequencies from different locations. Communications attorneys then file an application for that frequency and location with the Federal Communications Commission (FCC), the United States Government agency that regulates broadcasting. If and when the application is approved, the FCC issues a construction permit, an authorization to build a station at that specific location under certain terms and conditions. Additional consultants, engineers, and technicians plan and set up the station's transmitter and other facilities, all in compliance with the specifications of the construction permit. Architects, construction engineers, and contractors collaborate to build quarters that house the broadcasting, business, and technical activities of the station. Following the station's construction in accordance with the permit, the FCC issues a license to operate for a renewable term of 7 years.

Once on the air, a station is run by a chief executive, usually a general manager, who recruits and forms a group composed of managers that head up the station's programming, sales, and engineering departments. A commercial station seeks to attract an audience and advertisers, and, at the same time, preserve its broadcast license by operating within the law. To do so, it relies on its management group and a staff that consists of members who function as writers, production specialists, copywriters, account executives, traffic managers, promotional personnel, audio engineers, technicians, bookkeepers, librarians, clerks, and receptionists, and in other positions which support the efforts of disc jockeys, announcers, newscasters, sports reporters, and other on-air specialists. Each station also depends on the skilled personnel of networks, program services, consultants, regional and national sales representatives, advertising agencies, and other businesses for a myriad of services designed to enlarge its audience and improve its sales. Unquestionably, radio is a great deal more than disc jockeys.

From Jacks-Of-All Trades To Broadcast Specialists

Radio's first staff members were all engineers. They built and operated the experimental stations when the industry was in its infancy. They also provided all of the programming, serving as the original announcers. After some technical problems were solved in the 1920's, radio became a reliable medium of advertising in the United States, and it grew and prospered. Staff members of the original commercial stations and networks were jacks-of-all-trades who became adept at all aspects of the business through on the job training. They came to radio from many fields, including show business, advertising, and journalism.

Modern radio no longer relies on talent drawn from other fields. It produces its own professionals whose careers start in a farm system of educational, public, or hometown commercial stations. Except in small stations where jacks-of-all trades are still found, employees in commercial radio are specialists in the areas of programming, sales, engineering, and management. For each performer heard on the air, many people work behind the scenes to support his or her efforts. As a result, a relatively small percentage of radio employees are on-air performers. There is plenty of room in this field for a person who does not have the voice for radio.

Those who want to get into radio today generally try to match their talents, temperaments, and backgrounds with the jobs that complement them. Typically, an outgoing person with a good voice and a flair for show business is a candidate for an on-air position. One who has business and merchandising abilities usually is attracted by the work of the sales department and attempts to become an account executive. And a technically oriented person tries to become a member of the engineering staff. These are not hard and fast rules. Many staff members have started their careers in one department and wound up in another. For example, many sales persons began as on-air performers. Most management personnel are drawn from the ranks of sales, although some come from all other departments.

Breaking into radio is no simple task. The competition for each job, even in good times, is intense. Once the decision has been made to try to make it in the industry, a hopeful's immediate objective is to land a first job as an apprentice, learn enough to become a journeyman, and ultimately earn the status of broadcast professional. Once on the job, he is in the position to expand his knowledge of the industry and take advantage of the opportunities for advancement as they develop. No entry level job in radio is too menial if it provides one with valuable experience and opportunities to move into more meaningful positions. Many who began in radio with non-broadcast positions, such as messengers, receptionists, and bookkeepers, have gone on to great careers as broadcasters.

What Working In Radio Is Really Like

A commercial radio station is more than just a business, and working in radio is more than just a job. Every person associated with a station must have a clear understanding of the public service aspects of broadcasting in the United States. While each station has to produce a reasonable profit to survive, it must operate by law to serve "the public interest, convenience, and necessity." The satisfaction of these requirements should be the primary concern of the owners, managers, and staff members in all of their efforts on behalf of the station. A station's failure to comply with the rules and regulations of the FCC may result in the assessment of a heavy fine, and, in a serious case, a forfeiture of the station's broadcast license.

A career in radio can be both exciting and demanding. Each individual in the field should be competent and able to adjust quickly to changing situations. Survival amidst the many pressures of the business requires stamina. A successful broadcaster will generally have a lively interest in local, state, national, and world affairs, a love of the work, and the talent to grow within the field.

Formal training is ordinarily not required to land a first job at a small station. Certain aspects of radio may be learned only by actual experience in the field, but a broad, general education plus diversified radio experience are essential to prepare an individual to move on to jobs in larger markets and at the management level. To qualify as a broadcast executive, one must be a good manager, have the abilities to lead, encourage, and motivate personnel, and be able to diagnose trends within the station's market and the industry generally.

Radio compares favorably to many other fields in two important categories — pay and working conditions. With the exception of some major market on-air personalities, sales people are the best paid in the industry. They are usually compensated on a commission basis, and, as a result, receive remuneration which is in direct proportion to their success in sales. All other salaries of radio station employees vary in accordance with the size of the station and its market.

The radio industry offers great career opportunities to men and women of all races, religions, and national origins. An FCC policy specifically requires each station to maintain an affirmative action program and has greatly stimulated the hiring of women and minorities. Any applicant seeking an authority from the FCC to construct a new station or acquire control of an existing station is required to adopt a specific program designed to afford equal employment opportunity to all qualified persons and to refrain from discrimination in employment and related benefits on the basis of race, color, religion, national origin, or sex.

Radio still attracts many people who want to make it in show business. The local radio station is the most accessible entry point for an aspiring performer. A great number of persons who have succeeded in other branches of show business, such as television, motion pictures, and the theater, got their starts in radio. An individual seldom remains an employee of a hometown station for a long period of time. In order to advance in this business, you must be prepared to hit the road and move on to stations in larger markets.

I believe radio is a phenomenal career field, offering unlimited opportunities for creativity and individual achievement. No medium stimulates the imagination as radio does. By the use of voices, sounds, and music, radio is capable of producing any emotion and isolating any thought. It is by far the most personal of all media — capable of reaching a listener in his own environment at any time. Radio is portable and relatively inexpensive to transmit and receive. It is instantaneous, alive, flexible, and good company. Radio is all around all the time, and it provides something for everyone by means of diversified broadcast formats.

But you should not misconstrue my enthusiasm about the industry. Radio is not a career for everyone. Due to the nature of the competition for listeners, newsbreaks, and advertisers, just to mention a few, the atmosphere at a radio station is often pressured. Radio is a tough business, measured by ratings, renewals, and reviews. Survival often depends on hard, cold numbers. All staff members — whether on or off the air — are on the line each day. And visions of instant glory in the business are quickly dispelled by an on-air shift that starts at 4:00 A.M. or by efforts to make that first sale of commercial time to a businessman who never listens to the radio. Few experiences equal the unexpected chill felt by a staff when the sale of its station is announced, and nobody knows much about the new owners. A career in radio is seldom a "piece of cake," but what of real value in life ever is?

What This Book Will Do For You

Breaking into radio and succeeding in the field require a great deal more than being at the right place at the right time. A lucky opening may provide you with a great opportunity to show your stuff, but if you do not have the skills it takes to do what is expected, your stay on the job will be short-lived. But if you have the necessary *talent*, *drive*, and *knowledge of the field*, you can make it in this magical business when offered the chance to demonstrate your abilities. Over the long haul, cream rises to the top, and there is always room for the best in radio.

Talent is a special artistic or creative personal ability. It is a natural resource which, if not utilized, is wasted. But talent alone does not guarantee success in radio. We all know extremely talented people whose careers have gone nowhere. Achievements in radio, as in any other field, require hard work. There is no substitute. But hard work without proper direction is a futile effort. If you energetically plunge forward into a career without any knowledge of the environment in which you must compete, you are likely to end up on a treadmill to oblivion. All of your talent and hard work in combination with knowledge of the field of radio will help you to avoid that treadmill.

Making It In Radio is designed to be your key to a career in radio broadcasting. Its discussions of the principles, concepts, and workings of the commercial radio industry and the many jobs and careers it offers provide you with invaluable knowledge of the field that is essential for your success. A resource for anyone who wants to know about radio, either as a professional or for personal understanding, it reviews the history, size, importance, scientific theory, and regulation of the industry. Thereafter, the commercial radio station is discussed by examining the functions of its various departments and the skills needed to make them run. Throughout the book, the origins of the industry are explained in order to place modern radio and its regulation by the FCC into perspective. The future of radio, the wonders of satellite communication systems, and the rebirth of network radio are examined. Nineteen radio professionals, presently working in all phases of broadcasting, counsel you with first hand advice on how to determine if a career in radio is for you, and, if so, what you should do to prepare yourself for it, to get into the field, and to advance your career within the industry. Finally, a comprehensive glossary of the language of American radio is provided.

Few of the thousands of successful men and women now working in radio could have accurately predicted what they would be doing today when they launched their careers. Many began as weekend announcers, part-time technicians, and clerks in small hometown or college stations. As their knowledge of the field expanded through experience and new opportunities developed, they moved on to more responsible and lucrative jobs. They were ready to take advantage of the breaks as they appeared. As you start your career in radio, you also have no way of forecasting with certainty where your journey in the field will ultimately take you. We do know, however, that *knowledge of the field* now will greatly assist you in finding a place in radio and achieving your full potential in the industry. The more you know, the greater your chances are for success. *Making It In Radio* is a start. The rest is up to you.

Young "jock" on the air.

Chapter Two

The Development of Commercial Radio

Radio has become a huge industry that reaches more than 95 percent of all Americans every week and better than 75 percent each day. The average household contains six radios, including those in automobiles. At least 60 percent of the population is awakened each day by clock radios. More than $3.5 billion is spent annually on new radios, and there are more than 550 million sets located in homes, businesses, and vehicles.

Radio is a vital force in the United States. Over 8,000 commercial radio stations provide their audiences with diversified information and entertainment. Every time an American turns on a receiver, he joins an average listening audience of more than 30 million. Radio reaches more people daily than television, newspapers, or magazines. It is America's around-the-clock constant companion and is still growing. The industry's total audience, number of stations, and gross revenue have increased each year since the early 1960's.

Commercial radio is an integral part of the free enterprise system. While stations are prohibited from transmitting obscene, indecent, or profane language, or information concerning lotteries, and are subject to the laws of libel and slander, they are otherwise unrestricted in what they may broadcast. As a result, commercial radio is continually competitive, often beautiful, occasionally vulgar, but always changing and developing.

The freedom of American commercial radio stands in marked contrast to the controlled and censored programming produced in countries where radio is nothing more than the official voice of the government. In such countries, radio broadcasts what the government wants the population to hear and believe, and little else. Radio affects listeners' attitudes and behavior by influencing their thought processes; thus a free, privately owned radio system constitutes a threat to any regime which subordinates the rights of the individual to the needs of the state.

Modern radio has evolved into a highly believable and reliable medium. It has been informing listeners about every conceivable aspect of life since its inception. Whenever an extraordinary event occurs, Americans instinctively turn to radio first to get the facts. Whether the story is one of national interest or only important in a local area, radio informs, explains, questions, calms, advises, and serves the general public in many other ways. Radio even prevents injuries and saves lives. During the Northeastern blackouts of the 1960's and 70's, commercial radio, through fast, accurate, and informative reporting, dispelled the fears of millions and prevented chaos.

American commercial radio is a system of stations and networks that derive revenue from advertisers who wish to reach audiences with messages about their products, services, and ideas. The stations and networks charge advertisers to broadcast the messages which are called *commercials*. Because of its penetration, flexibility, and efficiency, radio sells effectively and has had a great impact on the national economy. Leaders in the fields of business, industry, and entertainment use radio as a primary tool in marketing on the local, regional, and national levels. The constant evolution and refinement of radio formats allow advertisers to select those stations whose audiences are most likely, based on categories such as age, sex, education, and income levels, to respond positively to their commercials.

Radio — The Product of an International Effort

Radio was developed through the theories, experiments, discoveries, and inventions of many brilliant people of different nationalities. In 1864, James Clerk Maxwell, a Scottish scientist, who is considered one of the great mathematicians and physicists of the 19th century, identified light with electrical energy and predicted the existence of radio waves. His work was based on the earlier discovery of electromagnetic induction by the English chemist Michael Faraday.

The actual production of electric waves in 1887 by Heinrich Rudolph Hertz, a German physicist, made possible the development of radio, television, radar, and all of the other related electromagnetic wonders. Hertz determined that rapid variations of electric current can be projected into space in the form of waves (then called Hertzian waves) similar to those caused by light and heat. He was first to create what are now called radio waves. His work has been honored by the adoption of the term "hertz" (Hz) as a unit of frequency equal to one cycle per second by the international scientific and engineering communities.

Using the theories and apparatus of Hertz and the discoveries of Edourd Branley of France, an Italian inventor and electrical engineer named Guglielmo Marconi produced the first practical wireless telegraph system in 1895. Prior to that time, all telegraphic messages had to be transmitted through cable which severely limited the use of this form of communication. His breakthrough was a major element in the development of radio which for years thereafter was known as the

Communications pioneers gather at RCA's experimental transoceanic station in New Jersey in 1921. The group, from left to right, included: first three men unidentified, David Sarnoff, Thomas J. Hayden, Dr. E. J. Berg, S. Benedict, Professor Albert Einstein, Nikola Telsa, Dr. Charles P. Steinmetz, Dr. Alfred N. Goldsmith, A. Malsin, Dr. Irving Langmuir, Dr. Anthony W. Hull, E.B. Pillsbury, Dr. Saul Dushman, R.H. Ranger, Dr. G.A. Campbell, Ernst F.W. Alexanderson, last man unidentified. *Courtesy of RCA.*

"wireless." On September 12, 1901, Marconi successfully completed the first transatlantic wireless signal in history, a message from Cornwall, England, to St. John's, New Foundland. He was also first to demonstrate that wireless or radio signals travel greater distances at night than during the day. For their independent work in the development of radio, Marconi and Karl Ferdinand Braun, a German physicist, shared the 1909 Nobel Prize in physics.

Marconi's historic broadcasts consisted of messages in Morse Code, transmitted by short bursts of direct electrical energy. Two inventors, Reginald Aubrey Fessenden, a Canadian professor, and Ernst Alexanderson, a native of Sweden, collaborated to give radio its ultimate dimension — the ability to transmit and reproduce the human voice, music, and other sound faithfully. They built a device capable of creating an alternating current whose fluctuations occurred so rapidly that they were above the range of the human ear. They sent the alternating current to an antenna and produced radio waves which carried sound. On Christmas Eve, 1906, Fessenden broadcast what is believed to be the world's first radio program when he delivered a short speech, played a selection on the violin, read a short religious passage, and played a phonograph recording from Brant Rock, Massachusetts. Radio operators aboard ships in the Atlantic, accustomed to hearing dots, dashes, and static through their headphones, were shocked to hear voices and music.

Lee DeForest, an American inventor, is considered by many as the "father" of modern radio for his work in both the development of the technical aspects of radio and its use as a viable medium of communication. He is credited with the first practical utilization of the vacuum tube which creates, strengthens, combines, and separates the electronic currents or signals required in the operation of radio. The vacuum tube was invented by Thomas A. Edison in the 1880's, but he did not grasp the importance of his find. DeForest realized that the functions of the vacuum tube were essential in the development of long distance radio transmisions. In 1906 and 1907, he patented vacuum tubes called the "audion" and the "triode." Many scientific historians consider the development and utilization of vacuum tubes by DeForest to be equal in importance to the discovery of radio waves by Hertz.

Edwin H. Armstrong, the brilliant American inventor and professor of electrical engineering at Columbia University, contributed much to the advancement of radio. During World War I, he perfected a device that detected approaching aircraft by picking up electromagnetic waves sent out by their engines' ignition systems. A modification of this device became the superheterodyne circuit which vastly improved radio receivers. Armstrong is believed to have developed many radio innovations which were stolen by others. However, his greatest contribution, and the invention to which his name will forever be linked, is a system of static-free broadcasting known as frequency modulation or FM.

Radio — How It Works

The development of communications by electromagnetic radiations traveling at the speed of light — radio — is one of the most remarkable achievements of science in the 20th century. Radio has thousands of practical applications in many fields such as science, medicine, industry, and business. The terms *radio* and *broadcasting*, as used here, mean the transmission of sound by amplitude modulation (AM) and frequency modulation (FM) stations for reception by the general public.

Radio works by converting sound into electromagnetic waves, also called radio waves, which travel at 186,000 miles per second. When they reach a radio receiver, radio waves are transformed into the original sound. For example, as an announcer speaks in a studio, his voice creates sound waves which cause vibrations inside a microphone. An electrical current running through the microphone is disturbed by the vibrations. The disturbances in the electrical current create electric waves that match the original sound waves. The electric waves so produced are sent through a control board at the radio station to the transmitter which simultaneously creates another type of wave called a "carrier wave." The transmitter greatly strengthens the electric waves and combines them with the carrier waves to form the radio signals which are to be broadcast. The transmitter delivers the radio signals to the station's antenna which sends the radio signals into the atmosphere in the form of radio waves. The radio receiver then picks up the radio waves and transforms them into carrier waves and electric waves. The carrier waves dissipate, but the electric waves are further transformed into sound waves by creating vibrations in a loud-speaker which match the vibrations originally made in the microphone.

All radio starts with electricity. No one knows why electricity acts as it does. Scientists classify heat, light, and electricity as forms of energy. They are not different energies — they are variations of the same thing. Simply stated, electricity is made up of several kinds of tiny particles. Some of them are positively charged, some negatively charged, and others are neutral. The negatively charged particles — *electrons* — are vital to radio.

An electric current is basically a stream of electrons which are moving. The electric currents used in radio consist of billions of electrons per second. An electron, moving by itself, is a minuscule amount of energy. To keep a 100 watt, 120 volt tungsten light bulb lit for one second, about 5.3 quintillion electrons (5,300,000,000,000,000,000) must pass through its filament.

Electric currents are either direct or alternating. A direct current is a stream of electricity that always flows in one direction. An electric current which regularly reverses its direction of flow by constantly surging back and forth is an alternating current. Alternating currents can be made to reverse their directions at rates that vary from a few times per second to many billions of times per second. Electric currents used in AM radio alternate their directions from 540,000 to 1.6 million times per second, and the range of alternations in FM is 88.1 million to 107.9 million times per second.

Each complete alternation of an electric current is called a *cycle*. The number of cycles which occur per second is the *frequency* of the alternation. Radio frequencies are, therefore, identified by and distinguishable on the basis of their number of cycles per second. As we have seen, the modern term for cycles per second is the *hertz* (Hz).

High frequency alternating currents are used in radio because such an alternating current flowing through a broadcast antenna produces an electromagnetic field in space that has the same frequency as the frequency of the alternating current. That field is radiated by pulses into space which travel at the speed of light — over 186,000 miles per second. Because these pulses are radiated one after another and are similar to waves in water, they are called *electromagnetic waves* or *radio waves*. Until the 1940's, radio waves were classified by their respective *wavelengths*, the distance in a line between the crest of one wave to the crest of the next wave. The wavelength has given way to the frequency as the standard by which each radio station is distinguished.

The frequency and power of each radio station are measured in hertz (Hz) and watts (W) respectively. The numbers used to describe frequency and power are very large, making it quite cumbersome to keep track of the zeros. As a result, the following standard prefixes are universally employed when refering to frequencies and amounts of power of radio stations:

kilo- = one thousand   Symbol: k
      Examples: 1300 kHz = 1,300,000 hertz
              50 kW = 50,000 watts

mega- = one million   Symbol: M
      Examples: 92.7 MHz = 92,700,000 hertz
              5 MW = 5,000,000 watts

giga- = one billion   Symbol: G
      Examples: 3GHz = 3,000,000,000 hertz
             10GW = 10,000,000,000 watts

The frequency of the radio waves produced in space is controlled by the number of the alternations of the current in the transmitting antenna of the station. The FCC assigns a specific frequency when it grants a license for an AM or FM station. The station is required to stay very close to the exact frequency and not to exceed assigned maximum power so as not to interfere with other stations. For example, if the FCC assigns the frequency of 92.7 MHz and maximum power of 3 kW to a new station, it must strive, whenever it is on the air, to broadcast at 92.7 MHz, and not 92.5 MHz or 92.9 MHz, and may not exceed 3 kW power.

Audio signals are superimposed on the radio waves and transmitted at the assigned frequency. The radio set (receiver) is designed to receive and then sort out the radio waves. It picks up the waves by means of its own antenna or aerial. The aerial is actually bombarded with radio waves transmitted by a number of stations at many different frequencies. The tuning of a receiver is accomplished by changing the capacitance of a circuit connected to the aerial. When correctly tuned to the desired frequency, the circuit allows in only the program on the selected frequency and excludes all others.

When received by the radio set, the waves are quite feeble. Within the receiver, the waves are greatly amplified, and the message carried by the original audio signals is reproduced by the loud-speaker.

The History of American Commercial Radio

The initial practical use of radio voice transmissions was in ship-to-ship and ship-to-shore communications. The first known sea rescue involving radio took place in 1909 when the *S.S. Republic* collided with another ship in the Atlantic Ocean. Radio messages sent by the *Republic* resulted in the rescue of most of its passengers. On April 14, 1912, David Sarnoff, a 21 year old wireless operator in New York City, received distress signals from the *S.S. Titanic*. Staying on the job for 72 hours, he transcribed reports which contained the names of survivors and descriptions of the disaster. For his efforts, Sarnoff received considerable acclaim. He went on to a distinguished career as a pioneer of broadcasting and the guiding force of Radio Corporation of America (RCA), the parent corporation of The National Broadcasting Company (NBC). The *Republic* and *Titanic* events demonstrated to all the importance and necessity of instant communications. Thereafter, radio's use developed rapidly in shipping, public safety, the military, aeronautics, industry, and many other areas.

In 1910, Lee DeForest dramatically demonstrated radio's ability to entertain by producing a live broadcast that originated from the Metropolitan Opera House in New York City and featured a large cast that included the opera immortal Enrico Caruso. This historic program and

Young David Sarnoff on duty at the radio station atop the Wanamaker store in New York. He stayed at his post 72 hours to report the S.S. Titanic disaster. *Courtesy of RCA.*

David Sarnoff and Guglielmo Marconi in 1933 at the RCA transmit-ting center at Riverhead, Long Island. *Courtesy of RCA.*

other early voice transmissions received much acclaim and whetted the public's appetite for more free entertainment from "the talking box."

Experimental radio stations went on the air at the University of Wisconsin in Madison in 1915 and in Pittsburgh in 1916. The identity of America's first commercial radio station is the subject of much debate. Many believe that KDKA in Pittsburgh, which grew out of an experimental station that began operating in 1916, has that distinction. Others think that the honor belongs to WWJ in Detroit which went on the air on August 20, 1920. Most broadcast historians agree, however, that professional broadcasting began with the KDKA broadcast of the presidential election results on November 2, 1920, when Warren G. Harding defeated James M. Cox. This event set off a national radio mania. The Department of Commerce was swamped with requests for broadcast licenses, Americans rushed out to buy radios, and newspapers started to print lists of the programs scheduled for broadcast by radio stations. But KDKA did not receive its broadcast license until November 7, 1921. WBZ, then in Springfield, Massachusetts, and now in Boston, was granted the first broadcast license issued by the Federal Government on September 15, 1921.

During the 1920's, radio stations began springing up throughout the United States. As early as October of 1922, the first rudimentary network was created when WJZ (now WABC) of New York City and WGY of Schenectedy, New York, broadcast the "subway World Series" between the Giants and the Yankees. The two stations were connected by telephone lines. Thereafter, a number of temporary networks were put together to cover special events. Twenty-five million listeners heard the inaugural address of President Calvin Coolidge in 1924 — a year in which Americans spent $358 million for radios. In 1926, RCA joined 24 stations by wires called *landlines* to form NBC, the first permanent national radio network. NBC accomplished its first coast-to-coast live broadcast, a play-by-play account of a football game, in 1927. In that year, the Columbia Phonograph Broadcasting System, later to become the Columbia Broadcasting System (CBS), was formed. The Mutual Broadcasting System (MBS) began to organize as a network in 1934. In 1941, the FCC adopted rules forbidding any organization or company from operating more than one network. NBC was forced to dispose of one of the two networks it was then operating. The network it sold in 1943 became the American Broadcasting Company (ABC). The FCC repealed the rules against multiple network ownership in 1968 at the request of ABC.

Until the 1950's, the four networks, ABC, CBS, MBS, and NBC, dominated radio throughout the United States. By 1960, their influence on the industry had declined to the point where they were merely news and sports services. As a result, each radio station became a medium of local communication and had to produce most of its own

Original studio and operating room, WBZ, Springfield, Massachusetts, in 1921. *Courtesy of RCA.*

programming. Additional background material about network radio and its resurgence in a modified form are discussed in Chapter Ten.

The Regulation of Radio

The early development of AM radio was rapid and practically uncontrolled. Stations broadcast on frequencies with little regard to the interference they caused to others using the same or adjacent frequencies. As a result of this serious situation, the infant commercial radio industry floundered perilously. Congress passed the Wireless Ship Act in 1910, but that legislation dealt only with the use of radio by ships. In 1912, Congress enacted the Radio Act which was the first domestic law intended to control the use of radio. It appeared that the Secretary of the Department of Commerce and Labor was granted the authority to regulate the stations and operators. As broadcasting moved from the experimental stage to that of commercial competition, it became apparent that the Radio Act's provisions were inadequate and that further regulation of the industry was crucial for it to survive. The first National Radio Conference called at the request of industry leaders in 1922 resulted in the issuance of additional regulations by the Secretary, but these also were insufficient to stem the complex problems that were arising from radio's unchecked growth. The National Radio Conferences called between 1923 and 1925 resulted in the adoption of regulations which established minimum and maximum power standards for radio stations and the allocation of the 550 to 1,500 kilocycles per second band for standard broadcast.

A series of court decisions in 1925 held that Congress had not granted the Secretary of Commerce and Labor the authority to regulate the radio industry. The Radio Act of 1912 was, in effect, dead. Some broadcasters immediately took advantage of this sudden lack of regulation. They changed frequencies, increased power, and extended the operating times of their stations although these actions caused considerable interference to other stations. The resulting situation was a crisis. At the request of President Coolidge, Congress enacted the Dill-White Radio Act of 1927 which created a five-member Federal Radio Commission (FRC) with the authority to issue radio station licenses, allocate frequency bands to various radio services, assign specific frequencies to individual stations, and control station power. The Secretary of Commerce was granted the authority to assign radio call signs (call letters), to inspect radio stations, and to examine and license radio operators. The clutter in the AM or standard band was so intense that 150 of the 732 then operating stations were permanently ordered off the air.

Although the FRC had succeeded in bringing order to the chaotic use of frequencies, it was apparent that some broader authority was necessary to regulate uniformly all local, interstate, and foreign communication by wire and radio, including telephone, telegraph, and broadcast. Recognizing this need, President Franklin D. Roosevelt directed the Secretary of Commerce to establish a committee to study all electrical communications. The committee recommended the creation of a single Federal agency with the full authority necessary to regulate all aspects of electrical communication. Adopting the recommendations of the committee, Congress enacted the Communications Act of 1934 (Act) which created the FCC, an independent Federal agency consisting of five commissioners appointed by the President with the advice and consent of the Senate.

Since its initial meeting on July 11, 1934, the FCC's primary function has been the enforcement of the Act, a piece of legislation that was modeled after the Interstate Commerce Act of 1887 which, in turn, was fashioned after the British Railway Act, adopted by Parliament in 1845. It is ironic that today's vast communications establishment, services, and technology are regulated under a statute whose origins predate the Civil War.

One of the FCC's responsibilities is the regulation of broadcasting. Its activities in this area fall into three categories. First, the FCC apportions the limited space within the radio frequency spectrum to all of the broadcast and non-broadcast needs which must be served. The radio spectrum is a limited natural resource. Demands for radio frequencies have increased tremendously with the development of technology. It is fortunate that new equipment and facilities have made previously inaccessible very high frequencies available for communications. Second, the FCC assigns frequencies to licensees in the AM, FM, and television bands. Frequency assignments are designed and computed so that each station operates within established FCC rules and does not unduly interfere with other stations. The broadcast license of each radio station sets forth the specific geographical location of its transmitting antenna, its frequency, maximum power, and hours of operation. Any deviation from these license specifications requires the approval of the FCC. Applicants for new stations must represent to the FCC that they possess the necessary legal, technical, and financial qualifications to operate a station properly. Each broadcast licensee is charged with the responsibility of serving "the public interest, convenience and necessity" under the Act. The manner in which the public interest is actually served is up to each licensee. Third, the FCC inspects and regulates radio and television stations so that they operate in accordance with its rules.

The FCC is forbidden by the express terms of the Act from censoring radio programs. Section 326 states: "Nothing in this Act shall be understood or construed to give the commission the power of censorship over the radio communications of signals transmitted by any radio station, and no regulation or condition shall be promulgated or fixed by the commission which shall interfere with the right of free speech by means of radio communication."

Every person associated with any aspect of radio broadcasting must abide by all FCC rules and regulations. Ignorance is no excuse. The necessity to comply with these rules and regulations cannot be over-emphasized. The FCC has the authority to assess penalities for infractions of the Act and its rules and regulations. A violating station is subject to penalties which include a reprimand, a fine, the issuance of a short term probationary license, or even the death sentence to a radio station — a license revocation or a denial of a license renewal. All actions by the FCC may be appealed within its structure and, thereafter, to the Federal court system.

The scope of this book precludes a comprehensive analysis of the regulation of radio stations and their operators by the FCC. Material on broadcasting and its regulation is available from the Public Information Officer, Federal Communications Commission, Washington, D.C. 20554. Lists of FCC publications sold by the Government Printing Office are also obtainable upon request.

Professor and Mrs. Edwin H. Armstrong with world's first portable AM radio. *Courtesy of Armstrong Foundation.*

Chapter Three

Characteristics of Modern Commercial Radio Stations

Many of today's top broadcast executives broke into radio as salespersons, disc jockeys, or reporters. They moved up the career ladder into management positions by learning much more about the business than just how to sell time, host music shows, and deliver newscasts. Early in their careers, they realized that radio is a most exciting industry and an environment in which they wanted work. They developed a finely honed curiosity about all aspects of the field and absorbed as much knowledge as possible. Your career as a broadcaster will probably begin at a hometown station. As your trip up the ladder starts, you should understand the many different characteristics that distinguish commercial stations.

Radio stations come in two basic types — AM and FM — and in numerous classes, sizes, and shapes. They are located in thousands of places, have many types of names, and are available in a variety of flavors. Most of these distinguishing features are examined in this chapter. Radio station flavors, which are created by program formats, are discussed as part of the general subject of programming in Chapter Five.

Some of the following material is technical in nature. It is included to explain the bases of the characteristics discussed and to provide you with a reference source for the future. The material is, however, routine, everyday stuff to radio professionals. Time you invest now to grasp its meaning is well spent and will pay dividends in the future.

Two Basic Types of Stations — AM and FM

The *electromagnetic spectrum* consists of frequencies which range from a very few hertz to trillions of hertz. Remarkable advances in technology have greatly increased the number of frequencies available for use in communications. High frequencies, previously thought to be unuseable, are now in service. Clusters of frequencies within the spectrum have different characteristics. The portion of the electromagnetic spectrum referred to as the *radio spectrum* consists of those clusters used in the various forms of radio and related services. Each cluster is called a *band*. All of the frequencies within each band generally act in a similar fashion. The categories of frequencies within the radio spectrum are:

Frequencies of the Radio Spectrum

Classification	Abbreviation	Range
extremely low frequency	ELF	30 Hz to 300 Hz
voice frequencies	VF	300 Hz to 3,000 Hz
very low frequencies	VLF	3 kHz to 30 kHz
low frequency	LF	30 kHz to 300 kHz
medium frequency	MF	300 kHz to 3,000 kHz
high frequency	HF	3 MHz to 30 MHz
very high frequency	VHF	30 MHz to 300 MHz
ultrahigh frequency	UHF	300 MHz to 3,000 MHz
superhigh frequency	SHF	3 GHz to 30 GHz
extremely high frequency	EHF	30 GHz to 300 GHz

AM and FM radio make up but two of the various bands in use within the radio spectrum. AM is the pioneer radio system of commercial broadcasting. Originally called the *standard band*, AM extends from 535 kHz to 1605 kHz, placing it within the MF classification. All AM stations are assigned frequencies within the band beginning with 540 kHz. Each of the total of 107 AM frequencies or channels are separated by a space of 10 kHz. The following illustrates segments of the AM band:

kHz

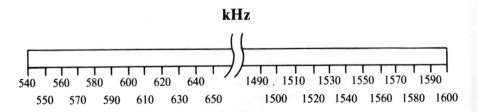

540   560   580   600   620   640   1490 . 1510   1530   1550   1570   1590
     550   570   590   610   630   650   1500   1520   1540   1560   1580   1600

While its principles were known to scientists and engineers for years, FM did not become a major force in commercial broadcasting until the early 1970's. Its frequencies are considerably higher than those of AM and are in the VHF classification. The FM band, which consists of 100 channels, starts at 88.1 MHz. Each succeeding frequency is 0.2 MHz higher, with the highest being 107.9 MHz. The 20 channels from 88.1 MHz to 91.9 MHz are reserved for noncommercial and educational use. The balance of 80 channels are assigned to licensees for commercial use. The following illustrates segments of the FM band:

MHz

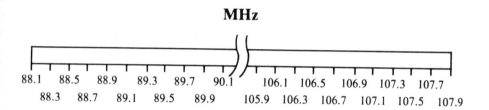

| 88.1 | 88.5 | 88.9 | 89.3 | 89.7 | 90.1 | | 106.1 | 106.5 | 106.9 | 107.3 | 107.7 |

88.1   88.5   88.9   89.3   89.7   90.1   106.1   106.5   106.9   107.3   107.7
   88.3   88.7   89.1   89.5   89.9   105.9   106.3   106.7   107.1   107.5   107.9

Sound is caused when molecules of air move back and forth in pulsating motions called *vibrations*. When these vibrations travel through the air to our ears, we hear them as sound or noise. Sound travels through the air at a speed of about 1/5th of a mile per second as compared to a rate of 186,000 miles per second for both light and radio waves. The higher the number of vibrations per second, the higher the pitch of the sound. The number of vibrations per second of each sound is also called its *frequency*. Normal human hearing is limited to sounds with frequencies between 20 and 20,000 vibrations per second. Each sound has its own frequency which is also expressed in hertz. For example, the lowest note of a piano has a frequency of 27 Hz, middle C's is 256 Hz, and that of its highest note is about 4,000 Hz.

In radio, the vibrations caused by sound or sound waves are converted into electric waves and superimposed on carrier waves. The carrier wave is the steady radio impulse generated by a station's transmitter on its assigned frequency within its band. The sound waves and carrier waves have separate frequencies. For example, middle C on the piano, at 256 Hz, broadcast at 95.1 MHz, "rides" on a carrier wave with a frequency of 95,100,000 Hz.

The term *modulation* basically means a controlled variation. In amplitude modulation (AM), the strength and size of the carrier waves vary to match changes in the electric waves produced by sound waves, and its frequency remains unchanged. On the other hand, in frequency modulation (FM), the frequency of the carrier waves change to match the changes in the electric waves produced by the sound waves, but its amplitude remains constant.

AM stations transmit sound with frequencies between 50 and 7,500 vibrations per second. Higher frequencies may be transmitted, but they produce *splatter*, or an overflow of signals that interferes with adjacent channels. No such problem exists in FM where the range of frequencies of sound transmitted runs from 30 to 15,000 vibrations per second. An electronic circuit created by Professor Armstrong gave FM the capacity to transmit sound with lifelike fidelity. It is generally free of static, inconsistent signals, and interference by other stations. The FM channel is wider than that used in AM, and it reproduces a broader and more dynamic range of tones.

AM and FM transmissions act differently in the atmosphere. The AM transmitter operates as if it were a floodlight which showers its immediate area with light. AM signals consist of both *groundwaves* and *skywaves*. The groundwaves travel through the air and follow along the contour of the earth's surface. The skywaves shoot upward into space. At night, the *ionosphere*, or the *Kennelley-Heaviside layer*, a collection of electrons a distance of 50 to 200 miles above the surface of the earth, reflects the skywaves back to earth, greatly extending the reach of AM stations. During the daytime, the ionosphere is ineffective, and AM signals are delivered almost entirely by groundwaves. Since they are more dependable, groundwaves have been designated by the FCC as the *primary signals*. Skywaves are classified as *secondary signals*. Many AM stations are required to reduce the power of their transmitters at night because the skywaves produced by their daytime power would cause substantial interference to other distant stations operating on the same or adjacent frequencies.

The FM transmitter operates much like a search light on a tower that shoots a circular beam of light into the distance, but does not illuminate the area around the tower. The FM signal travels through space along the line-of-sight to the horizon and does not follow the contour of the earth. FM signals pass through the ionosphere and are relatively constant during both day and night hours. Due to the "skip" produced at night by the ionosphere, high powered AM stations are capable of reaching greater distances than are FM stations of corresponding power.

Classes of Stations

By enactment of the Communications Act of 1934 (Act), Congress created the FCC to regulate all electric communications and to make possible "to all the people of the United States a rapid, efficient, nation-wide, and world-wide...radio communications service with adequate facilities at reasonable charges..." Thereafter, the FCC established various classes of radio stations for two important reasons.

First, the FCC recognized that the various areas of the country require distinctive types of radio service due to differences in population density and geographical features, such as conductivity. For example, many lower power stations are needed to serve the heavily populated, hilly areas of the Northeast. But sparsely inhabited, vast, and flat portions of the Midwest and Southwest regions require fewer, more powerful outlets. Second, the radio spectrum is a natural phenomenon, and each of its bands contains a limited number of frequencies. The manner in which each frequency in the AM band is used determines the number of stations across the nation to which that frequency may be assigned. In radio, the power radiated by an antenna determines both a station's area of coverage and the distance at which one station will cause interference to another on the same frequency. If a station transmitted at 1230 kHz with power of one million watts, it would cause interference to any other station using that frequency within a thousand miles of its transmitter. More than 170 stations in the United States are presently broadcasting at 1230 kHz because the power of each is limited to 1,000 watts daytime and 250 watts nighttime.

The stations within the classes provide local, regional, and extra-regional radio service. With only 107 AM and 100 FM channels with which to work, the FCC uses its classification system as a guideline, but ultimately assigns each channel and sets limits on power and hours of operation to provide maximum service to the general public with a minimum of interference to other existing stations.

The FCC has created the following four major classes of AM stations:

1. *Class I* stations operate on *clear channels* with a maximum of 50 kW and a minimum of 10 kW of power. Clear channels were created to provide primary and secondary broadcast service to both large urban and remote rural sections throughout the country during the nighttime. Only one or two Class I stations are authorized to operate fulltime on each clear channel. As a result, a nighttime clear channel signal covers half of the nation. Some directional, lower power stations may be assigned clear channels for daytime use only. In recent years, efforts to modify the rules relating to clear channels have resulted in the authorization of additional lower power AM stations on these frequencies. The AM band now contains 45 clear channels.

2. *Class II* stations are secondary clear channel facilities. They also serve large land areas and heavy population centers, but they are operated so as not to interfere with major clear channel stations. The AM band contains 29 channels assigned for use by Class II stations. They usually operate with daytime power of 50 kW to 10 kW, but as little as 250 W nighttime.

3. *Class III* stations provide broadcast service to population centers and adjacent rural areas on 41 regional channels. They operate with power not exceeding 5 kW daytime and one kW nighttime. More than 2,000 Class III stations now use regional channels throughout the United States.

4. *Class IV* stations provide limited broadcast service. They operate on local channels with a maximum power of 1 kW daytime and 250 W nighttime.

For the purpose of allocating frequencies within the FM band, the FCC has divided the United States into three zones. Zone 1 consists of 18 Northeastern states and the District of Columbia; Zone I-A is Southern California, and Zone II includes the rest of the country. Three classes of FM stations have been created:

1. *Class A* stations are intended to provide local broadcast service. They operate with a maximum effective radiated power of 3 kW and antenna height of not more than 300 feet above average terrain.

2. *Class B* stations operate with a maximum effective radiated power of 50 kW and antenna height of not more than 500 feet above average terrain.

3. *Class C* stations operate with a maximum effective radiated power of 100 kW and antenna height of not more than 2,000 feet above average terrain.

Class A stations are assigned to all zones. Class B stations are assigned to Zone I and IA, and Class C stations are assigned to Zone II.

The effective radiated power of an FM station is determined by a computation involving its antenna height and the power output of its transmitter. Under certain circumstances, the FM antenna height restrictions of the FCC are waived as long as the station's power output is adjusted to compensate for the additional height. In AM, the power of a station is measured by the actual power put out by its transmitter.

Locations and Shapes of Stations

"Where is your favorite radio station located?" is a question with more than one correct answer. Most of us tend to associate a station with the population center it serves. Its studios and transmitter site may be miles from a major area, but it will be considered a city station if it is received easily at "midtown."

Each station is required to identify itself on the air at sign on, sign off, and hourly, as close to the hour as feasible at a natural break in the program. According to FCC rules, the official *station identification* to be used at these times consists of the station's call letters followed by the name of the community or communities (also called "city of license") specified in its license as the station's location. If a station is licensed to a small suburban town but also serves a major market, its legal station identification must contain the name of the small town only. Some stations are authorized to use a "dual ID" and announce two locations on the air.

A mailman, asked about the location of a particular radio station, will probably answer by stating the street address of its main studios and offices. This is the place where the disc jockeys, sportscasters, and office staff work and, of course, where the mail is delivered. It follows, to him, that this is the station's location.

To most listeners, the location of a radio station has little to do with its city of license, station identification, or the address of its studios. They believe that the AM and FM bands are audio neighborhoods in which all of the radio stations serving their area are found. As a result, the address of each station is the specific spot on the dial where it can be found and heard.

A consulting engineer, whose concern is the power and shape of a station's signal, thinks of its location as that geographical area over which it has an exclusive license to use a specific frequency. Dozens of radio signals may be transmitted by other stations over the same territory, but they do not interfere with each other because each is assigned a different frequency. It's as if they all occupy the same office building, but each has its own floor.

The shape of a radio station is the pattern or contour of its signal. Each station's pattern is either nondirectional or directional. A nondirectional signal is authorized by the FCC when it will not interfere with any other stations operating on the same or adjacent frequencies. Directional signals are necessary to avoid such interference. A nondirectional signal acts like the ring created when a stone is dropped straight down into a pond of water. The ring or wave leaves from the point at which the stone enters the water. It forms a perfect, ever widening circle, and continues to the edge of the pond. Directional signals create patterns of irregular shapes. They are produced in the transmitting antenna. Multiple radiating towers are used in AM radio to create the desired directional patterns. They are placed in a particular array so that some of their radiation cancels or reenforces the signal as desired.

Due to the nighttime skywave feature of AM radio, most full-time AM stations are required to reduce power and operate with a directional signal after sundown. Almost all established FM stations are nondirectional, but some recently authorized stations are directional to protect other stations on the same or adjacent frequencies.

Antenna height is not an important factor in AM radio since the groundwave is the primary method for delivery of the signal. The whole structure — usually a tower — acts as an antenna and is cut to the size of the AM frequency. In FM, the height of the antenna is critical. The FM signals follow the line-of-sight, and delivery of the transmission depends on the location of the receiver in relation to the transmitter. While the FM antenna can be very short, it is generally placed on top of a tall manmade structure or a mountain. If the FCC approves an FM antenna height that is higher than that which is allowed for the class of the station, its power must be reduced proportionately to protect the signals of other stations and stay within the effective radiated power limits of its class.

Names, Slogans, and Symbols
By Which Radio Stations Are Known

Look closely at any successful American business that serves the general public. You quickly discover the elements of its success: good products or services, competitive prices, the capacity to satisfy a broad-based demand, management and production know-how, and familiar names, slogans, and symbols that cause instant recognition of the products, services, or company in the minds of its customers. The use of symbols to identify businesses and what they sell began in the 18th century when metalsmiths impressed "hallmarks" on products made of gold and silver. Since then, the success of a product or service in the marketplace can be measured by the degree of public recognition its names and symbols receive. People believe that a *familiar* brand is a *dependable* brand.

A commercial radio station is a business whose existence depends upon its instant recognition by listeners and demand for its service. A station that attracts an audience will attract advertisers. But one of management's most difficult tasks is impressing upon the listener's memory both the station's identity and the service it renders. Every day, each potential listener hears and sees countless names, marks, and symbols in advertising for hundreds of products and services. In addition, radio listeners seldom give any station their undivided attention because they are generally involved in other activities, such as driving, working, or reading, as they listen to radio. Each station must develop ways to cause its audience to remember its name amidst all of the others used in advertising. Through the repetitious use of creative names, slogans, and symbols, management informs listeners of the identity of the station to which they are listening, causes them to recall the station, and builds a more positive image of the station in their minds.

The accurate recognition of a station by its audience is critical in the competition for ratings which are estimates of the size and characteristics of an audience. Ratings are based on information obtained from a small percentage or sampling of the total audience in a market. Each listener who provides information to a rating service is, therefore, representative of hundreds of listeners in a given survey. Each station must carefully select names, slogans, and symbols which clearly distinguish it from all of the others in the market. Any confusion concerning the names or identity of a station could cost it valuable rating points, and lost rating points mean lost dollars.

A radio station's formal name is its *call letters*. They are chosen by a station's owners and assigned by the FCC if they are available and are not likely to be confused with those used by other nearby stations. Under international agreements, call letters of stations in the United States begin with W or K, in Canada with C, and in Mexico with X. Call letters assigned to stations east of the Mississippi begin with W and those west of that point start with K. A few pioneer stations such as KDKA, Pittsburgh, and KYW, Philadelphia, are exceptions to this rule. While some of the call letters assigned in the early days of radio contained three letters, such as WGN, Chicago, WBZ, Boston, and KNX, Los Angeles, those now assigned by the FCC contain four letters.

The call letters of established stations have great value due to their instant recognition throughout the country. WNEW, WOR, and WQXR, New York, KDKA, Pittsburgh, and KMPC, Los Angeles, are in this category. Those that spell an actual word, such as KOOL, Phoenix, WILD, Boston, or WIND, Chicago, are in demand. Others which are pronounceable contractions of words such as "kiss" — WKSS, Hartford, and KIIS, Los Angeles, and "magic" — WMGK, Philadelphia, have considerable worth. Those that describe a city, format, or entity are also prized. Examples of these include; WACO, Waco, Texas, and WARE, Ware, Massachusetts; KABL, Oakland, and KFOG, San Francisco, both of which relate to certain aspects of the Bay Area; KJAZ, Alameda, and KJZZ, Anchorage, both of which have used a Jazz Format, and WABC, WCBS, and WNBC, which are New York City based flagship stations of three major networks.

The names, phrases, and symbols used by some stations are based on aspects of their operations other than call letters. It is common for a station to adopt a name, slogan, or symbol which relates to its assigned frequency. Since most listeners consider its address to be the dial location, a station has a genuine interest in using a name that describes where it can be found in an easily remembered way. Examples of this technique are as follows:

Frequency	Name
1300 kHz	AM 13
95.5 MHz	Radio 95 1/2
99.9 MHz	FM 100

Advanced technology made the manufacture of smaller radio sets possible. As portable and automobile radios became more compact, the average dial size decreased. Since most car radio dials are less than 4 inches long, the numbers painted on them are something less than precise locations of frequencies. As a result, stations have developed the practice of rounding up, down, or off the actual frequency numbers in their advertising and promotional activities. For example, 95.7 MHz becomes FM 96, and 1410 kHz is promoted as Radio 14.

Many stations employ slogans that convey the types of programming or formats they offer. Examples of some presently in use are:

> The Place For Easy Rock
> Music Of Your Life
> A Place To Relax
> All News All The Time

Stations also use slogans and logos which convey two or more ideas about their operations. These hybrid phrases usually indicate both the dial location and format information in the following fashion:

> NewsRadio/88
> Beautiful 92
> Rock 95 1/2
> All Talk 15

Commercial radio stations have their own answer to William Shakespeare's famous question, "What's in a name?" *Everything.* By the use of thoughtful combinations of formats, images, and all types of names, slogans, and symbols, successful stations have achieved instant recognition in their markets and beyond. Having established themselves as familiar, living entities to their listeners, they have gone on to become dependable and trusted old friends by consistently living up to their images and staying in character.

Chapter Four

Radio Station Management and Organizational Structure

Management should be a dynamic force that constantly takes a business to new heights by overcoming obstacles. The people of management have the responsibility of making things happen. They set the goals, make the decisions, and establish the policies. Management enlists, trains, and inspires a staff to operate the business. That staff implements the decisions and the policies of management. The plan by which the members of the staff are used within the business is called its organizational structure.

A commercial radio station is a business that operates in a highly competitive and technical industry. It is also regulated by the FCC. Each station needs good, aggressive, and enlightened management to survive in the midst of this complex competition, technology, and regulation.

Throughout your career in radio, you will constantly be dealing with the management of a radio station, network, or allied business. Since management will have an impact on your destiny in the industry, you should know something about what it does and how it works. This chapter is designed to provide you with a start toward an understanding of (1) the usual objectives of radio station management; (2) the qualifications and duties of the chief of management — the general manager, and (3) the various organizational structures used by radio stations.

The Objectives of Management

Commercial radio stations exist to provide the general public with diversified broadcast services. They are also private property, operated for and owned by individuals, partnerships, and corporations who expect to make profits on their investments. If making profits were the only objective of the managers of a station, their jobs would not be much more meaningful or challenging than similar positions in other industries. Management has the responsibility to direct and control the affairs of a radio station in a way that satisfies the diverse demands of its audience, owners, advertisers, employees, and the FCC. Since each of these groups is interested in different aspects of the station and its operation, management faces a tall order. It must run a successful radio station and, at the same time, try to keep everyone happy.

Under the Communications Act, the FCC is required to make the most efficient use of the frequencies in order to serve best "the public interest, convenience or necessity." In fulfilling its role, the FCC assigns frequencies to radio stations and regulates their use through a licensing procedure. It, therefore, exerts great continuing influence on the manner in which radio stations are managed and operated.

A radio station never owns its frequency. It has the exclusive right to use that frequency in its area for a term of seven years under certain terms and conditions, established by the FCC under the law. At the end of each term, a station must apply to the FCC for a renewal of its license. Failure by a station to operate within the terms of its license or the law will result in a censure, a fine, or a termination of its license. In the event of such a termination, the radio station actually ceases to exist — all that remains are some of its used electronic and broadcast equipment, office furniture, wires, and a lot of memories. Without that license, there is nothing else. Management must impress each staff member with the importance of avoiding any conduct which places the license of the station in jeopardy.

While no station may be run as if commercial success were its only objective, it cannot survive without income. A station is no ordinary business, but it is still a business. It must pay its help, rent, electric bills, and other operating expenses. Management's objectives are, therefore, quite clear: It must keep the station alive by protecting and preserving its license and, at the same time, make a profit.

The General Manager - Qualities and Qualifications

One person, a chief executive, usually called the *general manager*, is responsible for all aspects of the operation of a commercial radio station. Whether he is called the general manager, station manager, or vice president/radio division, etc., depends on whether he owns an interest in the station, the size of the station and its market, and whether the station is operated as part of a group of broadcast properties. Whatever the title, the chief executive must possess very specific qualifications to succeed at this job. He needs the professional, emotional, and physical equipment to meet the tremendous demands placed upon him by the FCC and the station's owners, audience, advertisers, and staff.

The radio business is constantly evolving, and the competition never lets up. The general manager is always on the firing line. While nothing assures one's making it as a general manager of a radio station, it is clear that a person with extensive broadcasting experience and a thorough knowledge of the industry has an excellent start toward succeeding at the job.

As we have seen, a commercial radio station is, at one time (1) a private business organized for profit; (2) a public service facility, and (3) a part of show business — all rolled into a single operation. An effective general manager should have special executive skills and broadcasting experience to run this unique entity. More than a little background in business administration is necessary.

A general manager should have a thorough understanding of all phases of the radio business. He needs to be able to draw upon a vast reservoir of knowledge to meet all of the situations which arise daily in the operation of the station. His capacity to cope with these situations is developed from working in many areas of the field and through his insatiable curiosity about every conceivable aspect of the industry. While he relies heavily on the members of his staff to assist him in those areas in which he has the least personal experience, little about the station escapes him.

Management can make things happen only if the staff of a radio station digs in and works. Without people, a station's programming, sales, engineering, and other departments will not function. No general manager has ever been able to do it alone. He must possess and exercise the leadership abilities necessary to motivate his staff, fuse all of the individuals into a winning team, and keep morale high. To do so, he has to be aware of and concerned about the attitudes and sensitivities of each staff member. He must nurture the staff's creativity and establish an environment in which each member strives to reach his full professional potential. The general manager must have the capacity to communicate with his staff and delegate responsibilities in order to achieve his goals.

A general manager must be an individual of high personal and professional integrity in order to earn the respect of his staff, the owners, and all segments of society with which he deals. He has to be completely dedicated to his profession, prepared to take criticism from all sectors, and capable of bearing weighty responsibilities. He must constantly be mindful of the magnitude of the power he wields through his station — the force to influence and persuade the station's listeners. They trust the station and rely on what it says. The ultimate responsibility of the general manager is to make his station worthy of that trust and to insure that its audience is never betrayed.

The Duties Of The General Manager

A general manager receives his authority to run a radio station from its owners. The responsibilities borne by the general manager are determined by the extent of that authority. Some owners prefer to make all of the basic decisions pertaining to the station and leave the implementation of those decisions to the general manager. Other owners confer regularly with the general manager on major decisions, such as changing programming or hiring a new national sales representative, discussed in Chapter Eight, but give him the full authority to run the station as he sees fit. In the discussion which follows, we shall assume that the owners have granted the general manager broad authority and freedom, and that he has assumed the full responsibility for every internal and external activity of the station.

The general manager is the mastermind, the boss, and the moving force of a station. It has been said that a great general manager does nothing, but knows everything. In order to know everything, he must assemble a staff he trusts and upon which he relies. Each staff member should not only know his job and perform competently, but he must thoroughly understand the standards of excellence demanded by the general manager. People must work closely and harmoniously as a team if a radio station is to achieve those standards of excellence. Any discord between staff members that interferes with the operation of the station will not be tolerated.

Whether he is appointed to the post from outside the station's organization or moves up through its ranks, a general manager comes to that position with some definite ideas about radio. He has the duties of establishing the goals, doing the planning, and adopting the policies and procedures that will achieve success on all levels for the station. The general manager relies on the heads of various departments to assist him in accomplishing these goals and meeting his responsibilities.

One of the most critical concerns of the general manager is programming, the product of the radio station. The head of the programming department — usually called the *program director* — is responsible for each sound that goes out over the air. He is an important member of the management team because the degree of financial success a station attains is in direct proportion to the success its programming achieves with its listeners and advertisers.

The general manager must know a great deal about programming. He is constantly concerned with industry trends and aware of any indicators pointing to new directions in programming. He also has to keep informed about his own station's product, including on-air personnel and format, as well as the products of the media with which his station competes. He must confer regularly with his program director in order to keep in touch with all changes which could effect the station's product and to plan for additional facilities, personnel, and other support necessary to meet the challenges from the competition. They also analyze the results of the ratings and create strategies designed to react to those results.

The general manager has to understand that there are other considerations concerning programming that are more important than profits. Radio has the power to influence, persuade, and motivate people — and the general manager should be concerned that the programming director wields this power for proper purposes and the good of the community.

The *general sales manager* is another important member of the management team. As the person responsible for all sales activities of the station, he has the job of keeping the general manager informed as to how the station's product is being received in the marketplace. The general manager usually makes himself available to help close any major sales or promotion deal which might require his personal involvement. They meet often in order to consider the status of sales in the local, regional, and national markets. They are also concerned about the general business climate and how it affects the radio business. In addition, they work together on the planning, establishing of goals, and creation of policies and procedures relating to the entire area of sales.

The general manager, program director, and general sales manager constitute the management team of a radio station. When this trio of executives functions as a unit, the result is a strong, balanced, and well managed operation. Each must have an understanding of the other's responsibilities and problems and be committed to working together for the accomplishment of the station's goals.

The *traffic manager* is the general manager's guardian of the raw material of the station — the 60 minute hour. He supervises all of the record keeping and execution related to the advertising sold by the station and prepares logs which serve as schedules for on-air personnel. The traffic function is important because it bridges the gap between programming and sales.

The *chief engineer* or an independent contractor performing the same functions is also a vital cog in the operation of a station. He reports directly to the general manager concerning the status of the station's signal, equipment, and record of compliance with FCC rules and regulations. Together they review technical and equipment innovations which may be employed to enhance the station's sound. They also consider, on a long range basis, major technical moves, such as the filing for an authorization to increase power or for permission to use a more effective transmitter site.

A general manager often relies on an *office manager* who supervises all of the general and administrative tasks which are important to the operation of the station. Personnel dealing with secretarial, filing, bookkeeping, reception, and other functions are handled at this level.

The list of the daily activities of a general manager appears to be endless. He deals with all types of programming, sales, engineering, and administrative problems as well as with unions, lawyers, accountants, bankers, consultants, organizations, regulatory matters, owners, and the community at large.

A healthy community is an environment in which a radio station thrives. A general manager usually does more than his share for the community by making himself and his clout available for worthy governmental, charitable, and civic activities. He is personification of the station — a symbol of its vitality, importance, credibility, and involvement. The successful general manager may do nothing, but it usually takes him at least 12 hours a day — and his work is never done.

Organizational Structures of Radio Stations

The success of any commercial radio station depends upon the competence, creativity, experience, and attitude of its people. Without a dedicated and capable staff, no station reaches its potential for public service, professional achievement, and financial return. Such a staff, the proper technical facilities in a viable market, a good frequency allocation, and adequate power are the elements necessary to build a respectable radio station. Management is the glue that bonds these elements into a winner. The system by which management establishes a chain of command and utilizes its staff is set forth in the station's organizational structure.

No two radio stations are organized in precisely the same manner. The structure of each depends on many factors such as size, program format, and market location. For example, a small station, which programs rock music, may operate a news division that consists of three people and is a part of the programming department. In another market, a small station, with similar technical facilities, which features a mix of adult contemporary programming, may have an independent news department, operated by a staff of eight.

The titles of management and staff people seldom fully reveal what they do within the radio operation. In smaller stations, it is common for a general manager to serve as either program director or sales manager or both. A salesman might also do the play-by-play announcing of the basketball games of a local college, and an evening talk show host might write promotional material or work in production during the day. The total staff of such a small station might consist of seven or eight people, each doing a variety of unrelated tasks. The smaller local station provides an excellent training ground for people beginning their careers in broadcasting. Due to the demands of the operation and the limited number of available people, the entire staff is compelled to work in almost all phases of the station's activities. It is here that broadcasting's last jacks-of-all-trades are found.

At larger stations, the functions of the management and staff positions are more specifically defined. Stations in larger markets are more complex and are generally organized by labor unions. The staff members tend, therefore, to become more specialized. The people of any station, large or small, must, however, be prepared to respond at a moment's notice to meet any emergency situation. By tradition, when the health and safety of the general public are involved, getting the job done and serving the audience of the station take priority over anything else. When the chips are down, Americans turn to radio and its radio professionals are there to serve.

Under optimum conditions, a general manager creates the organizational structure of a station with his goals and budget in mind. He visualizes the organization and all of its parts. The parts are then integrated into a working unit. A determination is made as to the number of types of staff positions necessary to make the organization work. The staff positions are then filled with the most able people available, and the standards of performance expected by the general manager are communicated to each member of the staff. Thereafter, the system is monitored and adjusted by the general manager as the results achieved by the organizational structure are measured.

A radio station is a living, changing entity which often operates in ways not shown by the neat, clean lines of the organizational chart. Those lines are occasionally bent in order to get a job done. While stations seldom rigidly adhere to their organizational charts, each must have a structure so that every staff member knows the general shape of the operation and to whom to report. When you land the first job in radio, you should study the nature of the station's environment. In time, you will understand who runs the station and how it is being done.

The following organizational charts demonstrate some of the possible structures used to operate radio stations in small, medium, and large markets. Keep in mind that the organizational structure of each radio station is unique.

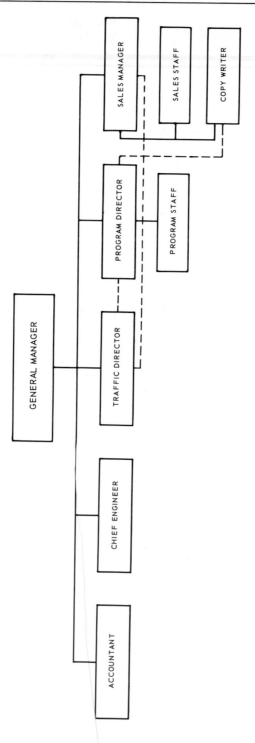

Organizational chart of typical radio station in a market with a population of less than 10,000. (From "Radio Station Organizational Charts," Copyright 1969 by National Association of Broadcasters. Reprinted by permission.)

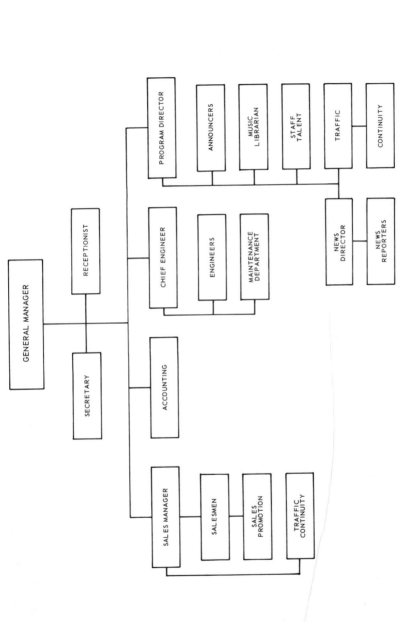

Organizational chart of typical radio station in a market with a population of 50,000 to 100,000. (From "Radio Station Organizational Charts," Copyright 1969 National Association of Broadcasters. Reprinted by permission.)

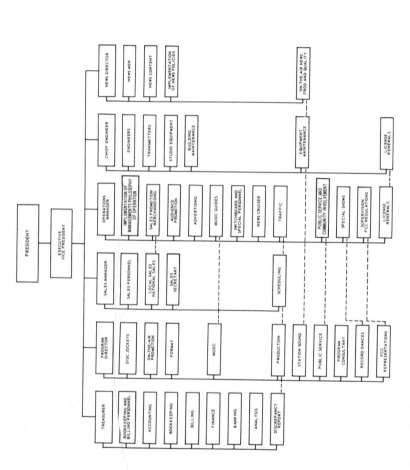

Organizational chart of a typical radio station in a market with a population of 2.5 million and over. (From "Radio Station Organizational Charts," Copyright 1969 National Association of Broadcasters. Reprinted by permission.)

Chapter Five

Radio Audiences and Programming

The essence of modern commercial radio is intense daily competition among stations in every market. They vie for advertisers, news-breaks, talent, and on every other conceivable level. But the ultimate contest in radio is the battle for the attention and loyalty of an audience — the people who regularly tune in and receive each station. In the struggle to attract and retain a radio audience, programming is the chief weapon.

Radio programming is an inexact art form, but its success in capturing and retaining an audience may be scientifically measured. Advertisers, who provide commercial radio stations with revenue, need to know who is listening to what stations and when before they make decisions to buy time. The popularity and profit of each station, therefore, depends upon the extent an audience accepts and approves of its programming. Accordingly, the creation of all programming for each station must begin with an understanding of the radio audience it is designed to serve.

Yesterday's Audience and The Golden Age of Radio

By the late 1920's, radio had solved its earlier technical problems, and stations were transmitting dependable signals. Full-time networks developed and immediately flourished. The industry had attracted a large national audience that was listening to its programming on a regular basis. Advertisers quickly realized that this mass medium was an effective way to sell their goods and services.

From its beginning to the early 1950's, prior to the emergence of television, commercial radio was the chief source of home entertainment in the United States. Families across the nation gathered in their living rooms around their radio sets night after night, listened to their favorite shows, and were entertained, informed, and influenced by programming.

The networks and sponsors tried to attract the largest general audiences possible. The programming they produced was intended to appeal to persons of all ages, backgrounds, and financial and educational levels. Each network was mostly concerned with the *quantity* of its own audience and those of its competitors. At certain parts of the day and night, however, programming was aimed at (1) the family, (2) women, (3) children, (4) all adults, or (5) men because these groupings of listeners were believed to dominate the general audience during different time periods.

The period from the 1920's to the 1950's will always be remembered nostalgically as The Golden Age of Radio. The networks dominated the industry by producing and providing radio programs that featured the best live talent available in show business. By delivering a national audience, the networks attracted large revenue from prestigious advertisers. They were, therefore, able to provide a great variety of high quality programming unaffordable by any single independent station.

The key to the success of an individual radio station was an affiliation with one or more of the national networks. In 1947, almost 97 percent of all radio stations in the United States were network affiliates. In order to become an affiliate, each station had to clear (make available) substantial amounts of its broadcast time for network programming and advertising. Through tough affiliation agreements, the networks greatly influenced what local stations programmed. Locally originated programs were used to fill in the few slots in each station's broadcast schedule not committed to network shows. Except in a few major markets, independently programmed radio stations were not much of a factor in the industry.

The radio programs during this period were usually 15, 30, or 60 minutes in length, but special broadcasts, such as descriptions of sporting events, were open-ended. The networks all relied on the same rudimentary audience research and made similar assumptions about that audience. Accordingly, the programs produced by the networks were essentially similar in format and style. Each program was broadcast live. The most successful program formats were:

Radio Drama - Heard during the prime evening hours, these dramatic productions were weekly anthology shows directed at an adult audience. The stories were either original scripts or those drawn from motion pictures, the stage, novels, or the classics. The nation's greatest dramatic stars, like Frederic March, Olivia de Havilland, and Clark Gable, regularly appeared on *Lux Radio Theater, First Nighter, The Mercury Theater,* and others.

Comedy, Variety, and Musical Shows - These prime time presentations, aimed at the family audience, featured reviews that were showcases for the greatest stars of the entertainment world. Some, like Bob Hope and Bing Crosby, were known first as stage and screen stars, and later as radio personalities. Others, including

Jack Benny and Fred Allen, became stars directly through this type of radio show.

Adventure, Crime, and Mystery Shows - These programs played in the "theater of the mind" in a unique manner. Some featured different characters and situations every week, while others had regular characters facing new situations in each broadcast. The plots dealt with law and order, mystery, adventure, and the supernatural. *The Green Hornet, Gangbusters, Charlie Chan,* and *Suspense* were a few of the more popular family favorites.

Soap Operas - Called soap operas because they were usually sponsored by the manufacturers of soap or related products, "soaps" were broadcast throughout the entire daytime. They were continuing, slow moving serials which dealt with the trials, tribulations, tragedies, and triumphs of people and their families. They were usually heard 15 minutes a day, 5 days a week, 52 weeks a year. Directed toward women, the soaps were housewives' constant companions. Memorable examples of these programs include *Our Gal Sunday, The Romance of Helen Trent,* and *Ma Perkins.*

Situation Comedies - "Sitcoms" were built around the funny things that happen to ordinary people at home, at work, or in school. Regular casts of characters did and said unpredictable things each week on these shows which became listening habits to millions of families. *Amos and Andy, The Goldbergs,* and *Easy Aces* were outstanding examples of sitcoms.

Children's Shows - Although directed toward children, these misnamed serials were the favorites of millions of adults, too. Modeled after continuing comic strips in newspapers, the programs featured heroics, escapes, and death defying adventures of main characters who managed to survive and appear in the "next episode" of shows like *Jack Armstrong, The All-American Boy, Superman,* and *The Lone Ranger.* They were broadcast three to five times a week during the late afternoon or early evening. *Let's Pretend,* starring Nila Mack, was known as radio's outstanding children's theater. For almost 25 years, it entertained and thrilled the very young with fairy tales every Saturday morning.

Quiz, Game, and Talk Shows - Billed as spontaneous and unrehearsed presentations, these shows were usually pitched toward adult or family audiences during early evening hours. Best remembered of these shows are *The Quiz Kids, Truth or Consequences,* and *Take It or Leave It (The $64 Question).* Talk shows of all types and descriptions were also aired for the benefit of this audience. The most successful featured show business gossip columnists like Hedda Hopper and Luella Parsons. Interview shows, such as the one presided over by Mary Margaret McBride for years, also retained substantial adult audiences.

News and Public Affairs - Radio was the first medium to deliver information to a mass audience about events as they were happening. Through regularly scheduled and special programs, the adult audience received reports and commentaries of local, state, national, and world importance. Lowell Thomas, H.V. Kaltenborn, and Edward R. Murrow were some of the pioneers of broadcast journalism.

Sports - The play-by-play excitement of national sports events was transmitted coast-to-coast by radio. Directed mostly toward men, these programs featured the World Series, bowl games, heavyweight championship fights, and many other events. Graham McNamee, Ted Husing, Bill Stern, Red Barber, and Bill Corum were some of the great names in sports from this era.

The object of all programming during the Golden Age was to attract as much of the total audience *at home* as possible. Since portable and car radios did not become common until after World War II, the home or household was the basic unit of audience measurement. By 1960, most audience measurements for radio were based on the number of people who listened rather than households tuned in.

Because research indicated that the early morning audiences of most stations consisted of farmers, agricultural reports became the traditional sign-on broadcast. Thereafter, from 7 to 9 A.M., the audience comprised entire families. While the head of the household was preparing to go to work and his wife was making breakfast, getting the children off to school, and planning her chores for the day, they all listened to the radio. Programming for this period included something for everyone: news, weather, information, sports, and entertainment.

Throughout the late morning, midday, and afternoon periods, much of the programming was directed at the American housewife as she toiled at home alone. For years, the middle segment of this period was called the "housewife's" hour. Each network programmed all of its soaps during this six to eight hour period every weekday in order to acquire that audience. In the late afternoon, a large children's audience was treated to episodes of adventure serials.

During the dinner hour, music, news, and informational programs were directed at the family audience until about 7 P.M. when adventure, crime, and mystery shows took over. The evening hours after 8 P.M. were filled with radio drama, comedy, variety, and music shows, and news and public affairs presentations, all aimed at the adult audience until 11 P.M. when local programming was broadcast.

Through its programming, each network attempted to deliver to its advertisers the largest percentage of the total number of households nationally listening to radio during any specific time period. Each network sought to produce the most desirable shows and feature the best known stars. Outstanding performers attracted their own followings to the networks' offerings and bolstered the all important percentage of audience delivered. The networks also engaged in counterprogramming, which is the scheduling of certain types of programs designed to attract a large portion of the audience from the simultaneously broadcast programs of competitors. For example, if at 9:30 P.M. on a given evening, Network A and Network B each programmed radio dramas, Network C might broadcast a quiz show or situation comedy then to draw away the audience of the other two networks.

Targeted Audiences and Modern Programming

By the start of the 1950's, some new developments radically changed the radio industry and its audience. Television was rapidly becoming America's primary source of home entertainment and, in the process, was taking over the formats of network radio. The sights and sounds of soaps, dramas, variety and musical shows, adventure programs, situation comedies, and all of the old features were now being delivered into America's homes coast-to-coast by the new television networks. Most of the radio networks' stars and production companies shifted to the new medium. At the same time, the number of radio stations on the air increased dramatically. In 1947, fewer than 1,000 were on the air. By 1960, more than 4,000 commercial AM and FM stations were in operation, and more were on the way.

The emergence of television and the rapid increase in the number of radio stations vying for local audiences and advertisers had a devastating effect on the radio networks. On November 25, 1960, CBS broadcast the last soap episodes ever heard on network radio. But long before that date, the era of network domination of radio and its audience had passed. Radio network programming had lost its ability to attract a large audience and, as a result, commanded fewer dollars from advertisers. The once mighty radio networks were no longer providing revenue to their affiliates. Instead, they had become minor programming services, delivering news, sports, and other specialty features. In 1937, the radio networks generated 50 percent of all radio advertising revenue. By 1960, they produced a mere five percent.

After the crash of network radio, most of the former affiliates became independent stations. Each soon realized it had a great number of hours to fill every day with local programming that would attract and retain an audience large enough to interest advertisers. Because few stations had the financial ability or staff necessary to continue the large live shows formerly produced by the networks, the industry developed the music and news format which is still used today. Local programming developed around disc jockeys and other on-air personalities. Their shows featured small talk, music from phonograph recordings, headline news and sports reports, and anything else that appealed to a large number of listeners and could be produced at a low cost. Every local station still sought to attract the largest share of the audience, but each began to devote some attention and research to better understand the type and quality of its audience.

Initially, the disc jockeys selected and played the music that they themselves wanted to hear. After a while, their personalities and tastes in popular music attracted large numbers of listeners. Thereafter, the listeners developed their own personal preferences for certain types of music. Music selection then became a more sophisticated matter and was done by a music director who supervised the record library and reviewed all new releases. As a result, various musical formats, such as Top 40, developed. As is the case today, each successful format was a programming formula that worked by consistently attracting and retaining a particular type of audience for a station.

Through the early 1960's, FM radio was used mostly to duplicate the programming of AM stations in a process called "simulcasting." In 1965, the FCC issued new rules which prohibited all licensees of AM-FM operations in markets with populations of 100,000 or more from simulcasting more than 50 percent of the time. With a great deal of additional time to fill, these FM stations built their separate programming around disc jockeys who, as was the case in AM, selected and played music they personally wanted to hear. The listeners attracted to this new FM programming eventually developed their own preferences, and, once again, new formats, such as Beautiful Music, were created.

By the end of the 1960's, the radio industry and its advertisers had finally rejected the concept that one homogeneous radio audience existed. Radio programming and advertising are now based on the premise that the total radio audience consists of a number of identifiable audiences, each of which comprises listeners whose needs and patterns of behavior are similar and who have *something in common.* Identifying an audience and ascertaining that "something in common" is what modern radio programming is all about.

Radio programming has become a highly complex, sophisticated, and perpetually changing undertaking. At some point, each station's owners and managers must decide, with a high degree of accuracy, just what group of listeners they plan to lure to the station through programming. That group is called the *targeted audience* because programming is aimed directly at its members with the intent of attracting and retaining them as listeners. People with biological, social, and economic characteristics in common, it is believed, share similar likes and dislikes in radio programming. As a result, typical targeted audiences today consist of groups of listeners who share one or more of the following characteristics: age, sex, education, occupation, income, lifestyle, race, religion, nationality, or spending habits. Some stations cater to the same targeted audience all of the time, while others serve different targeted audiences at various parts of the broadcast day.

The search for a station's targeted audience usually begins with a comprehensive analysis of its market and the total population served by its signal. Research, surveys, census data, and other sources provide valuable demographic information about the station's total possible audience. The analysis points out potential targeted audiences within the total population and indicates significant groups absent from the market. A station should not attempt to provide programming for listeners it does not reach. For example, if a particular station's signal does not cover an area where much agricultural activity takes place, its programming should not consist of large blocks of farm news.

After it has identified the potential targeted audiences within the market area of the station, management studies the targeted audiences and the programming of all the other stations with which it competes. It looks for a hole in the market — either a targeted audience not currently being served at all or one being served poorly by another station whose audience might be captured through similar, but superior programming.

The size and location of a market are also factors to be considered in the selection of a targeted audience. In a small, single-station market, the lone station is usually free to program whatever it wishes within reason and still retain its audience. While other signals may come into the market, the station probably has little competition because it is the only source of local news and sports coverage. In a major market with a large population, management is free to focus narrowly on a group with a specific lifestyle and still deliver a substantial number of listeners.

After considering all of the factors discussed above and many more, management selects the targeted audience the station will seek to attract. Whether a station has been on the air for 50 years or is signing on for the first time, the purpose of its product — programming — is to obtain positive reactions from those people to whom it is directed. Whatever group of listeners compose the targeted audience — men 25 to 49, blacks, or adults 35+, the programming must be created with the needs, aspirations, goals, and lifestyle of the targeted audience in mind. After choosing and implementing its programming, the station must monitor its results by analyzing the size, characteristics, and changing attitudes of its audience — information provided by various types of audience research.

Audience Research

The popularity and financial success of a radio station depend on the size and characteristics of its audience. Decisions regarding programming and advertising are based on information about the potential and actual audiences of each station. The geographical area in which listeners can receive a station is called its *coverage*. As we have seen, management selects its targeted audience based on many factors relating to the size and characteristics of the groups of listeners within its station's coverage. Critical information pertaining to these listeners is provided through audience research.

The group of listeners which actually receives a station at a given time is its *circulation*. Advertisers make their decisions to buy time on various stations primarily after ascertaining the number and characteristics of the people who make up the circulation of each. No station could ever prove that all of its listeners fit into its targeted audience because its circulation consists of listeners of widely different backgrounds, tastes, and economic circumstances. But a station can demonstrate its ability to deliver a substantial number of listeners who fit the profile of its targeted audience through credible audience research and evidence of the results obtained for its advertisers.

Since 1935, commercial firms have been in the business of conducting research and providing data about the programs of radio stations and networks. In that year, C.E. Hooper Company, using estimates based on telephone interviews, supplied information to subscribers about the number of homes that had radio receivers, how many households were using their receivers, what stations and networks to which they were tuned, and the percentages of listeners who could identify the names of advertisers.

In the mid 1960's, research firms started to provide more detailed audience information and demographic data, generically called *radio ratings*, not to be confused with "rating," defined below. This research has proven to be useful to buyers and sellers of radio advertising and to programmers. Businesses now select *targeted markets* for their goods and services by using many of the same techniques employed by radio stations when choosing their targeted audiences. Advertisers and their agencies place commercials on radio stations whose targeted audiences most closely resemble their targeted markets.

Audience research is used both to assist a radio station's sales effort and to help management make decisions and plans about the station's future course. Commercial research firms, such as Arbitron Ratings Company, estimate audiences by surveys based on diaries, telephone calls, interviews, and other means. These firms are paid by subscribing stations, networks, and advertisers to provide ratings reports or *books* based on surveys conducted from one to four times a year, depending

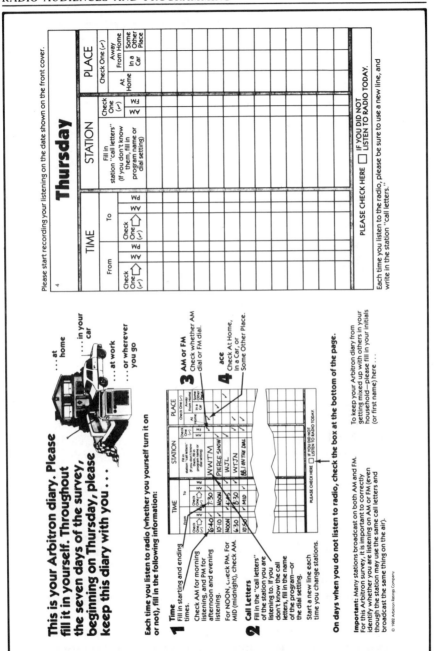

The sample Arbitron diary printed herein is fully protected by copyright and is the exclusive property of the Arbitron Ratings Company. Reproduction, in whole or in part, is prohibited without written permission from Arbitron.

on the size of the market. Each book defines the market geographically and indicates when certain categories of listeners tune to various stations during the average broadcast day. The categories consist of persons aged 12 plus, and men, women, and adults aged 18 to 24, 25 to 34, 35 to 44, 45 to 54, and 55 to 64, and in other groupings. Books also provide the following statistical data concerning each station:

Rating - The estimated percentage of the total population of a market that is tuned to a station. For example, if 1,000,000 people live in the Big City market, and 50,000 are tuned to radio station WXXX at a particular time, its rating is five.

Share - The estimated percentage of the aggregate radio audience actually listening to all stations in a market that is tuned to a particular station during some period of time. For example, if 500,000 people are listening to all of the stations in the Big City market, and 50,000 are tuned to WXXX at a particular time, its share is 10.

Cume or Cumulative Audience - An estimate of the total number of persons who tune in a radio station during a specified time period, such as a week or a month.

Trends - A comparison of a station's present book to previous estimates.

Commercial research provides basic information about who listens to what stations when, but it does not approach the question of *why* a certain audience is attracted to a specific station. The answer to that question must be determined by the management of each station through local research either obtained through commercial firms or performed by the station's staff. Person-to-person interviews, telephone inquiries, postcard surveys, shopping center samplings, and the like are the most common forms of research that assist management in making decisions about the station's future. Many stations now use "focus groups" to derive data. They consist of five or six people who participate in a discussion about their perceptions of a radio station. Their comments are recorded and evaluated by management and are helpful in shaping the image of the station. This type of data is usually considered secret and is not made available to advertisers, their agencies, or the station's competition.

The area of broadcast research and ratings is very complex and beyond the intended scope of this work. But it is important for you, as a radio professional, to keep in mind that the days when any commercial radio station can attract the public at large as its audience are gone forever. Increased competition forces each station to go after a narrower targeted audience which means continual reliance on sophisticated research.

Program Patterns and Formats

Radio programming consists of words, music, and sounds which entertain and inform the listener. Each segment falls into a recognizable category of programming such as music, news, sports, commercials, instruction, religion, agriculture, or others. The type, frequency, and tone of these segments are designed to suit the needs and desires of the targeted audience. The programmer is responsible for the establishing and maintaining a *sound* for the station that will acquire, please, and retain the targeted audience. The sound is, however, much more than a mechanical selection of segments. The goal of the programmer is to establish a unique sound that results from the special way the station blends the segments, produces its programming, and utilizes the creativity of its on-air talent.

After its sound has been established and put into effect, the radio station takes on a life of its own. Once the programming fixes an image or personality for the station, everything subsequently broadcast must be consistent with that image. In a sense, the station enters into an agreement with its audience. For its promise to maintain its sound consistently, the station's listeners agree to remain loyal and stay tuned. Should the station substantially depart from its sound, most of its listeners would consider that a breach of contract and tune to other stations.

Some stations present program segments throughout the day in a continuous pattern while others use different patterns in various dayparts. The patterns used vary from station to station. Most stations use one or more of the following four patterns:

(1) *All Music* - Designed to appeal to a targeted audience which likes a specific type of music to the exclusion of all others, the pattern may be used as a showcase for all types of music — running the full spectrum from beautiful to contemporary to classical. The musical segments dominate the broadcast day and are interrupted only for short periods for commercials, news, and brief comments.

(2) *Full Service* - This pattern consists of about 70 percent music, 10 percent news, 5 percent sports and special events, and 15 percent features. The type of music is generally in the adult contemporary or a middle-of-the road category, but the pattern works with almost any type of music. The targeted audience of a full service radio station usually is very loyal to the station and its on-air personalities.

(3) *All News* - The entire broadcast day under this pattern consists of segments of local, state, national, and international news, analyses of that news, reports concerning sports and weather, plus a number of features. Usually an affiliate of a national radio network which augments its news service, an all news radio station seeks to develop the

loyalty of the targeted audience whose members tune in at various times throughout the broadcast day to find out what's happening.

(4) *All Talk* This pattern consists of telephone call-in shows, panel discussions, interviews, and other audience participation productions, together with heavy news and sports coverage.

More than 80 percent of all radio programming today consists of music. It is, therefore, a critical element in the creation of a station's image and personality. After more than a quarter of a century of development, music formats have become highly sophisticated in order to meet the needs of identified targeted audiences. During the same time, non-music formats also evolved, and, as a result, the industry has developed certain shorthand phrases to define various formats. While the phrases or names employed are anything but precise, they are useful to national advertisers and their agencies. For an example, if an advertiser decides to buy the leading Rock station in each of the 50 largest markets in the United States, it would generally determine which station to buy in each market by checking one of the national publications, such as *Broadcasting Yearbook*, which lists all the commercial stations in the United States by formats. Unfortunately, many stations list themselves under a number of format names. Most time buyers are aware of this problem, but they cannot afford the time and money an independent analysis of each station's targeted audience would require.

Formats used by radio stations are constantly being redefined and reconstituted. While this area is not characterized by hard and fast definitions, the following represent some of the general format definitions usually accepted in the industry:

Adult Contemporary is the music of today, minus the most raucous tunes and abrasive talk (usually heard on rock stations), plus a mix of some old tunes, all presented in a full service pattern. A/C, a format mostly used on AM, is directed at a targeted audience of adults 25 to 49, and depends on bright on-air personalities and well produced news, sports, weather, and feature segments.

Beautiful Music consists of soothing, pleasant music drawn from movie sound tracks, Broadway shows, and standard ballads, performed mostly by string orchestras with an occasional vocal. Appealing to a targeted audience of adults 35 plus, beautiful music uses an all music pattern with limited clusters of commercials and news between 10 to 12 minute periods of uninterrupted music. The format is mostly found on the FM band.

Country varies in each geographical area. The music is a mixture of contemporary country music with roots extending to Hillbilly, Grand Ole Opry, Mountain Music, and Blue Grass Music, but uses modern techniques, instruments, and arrangements, and is rock oriented. The handling of news and features varies by the market, and the format appeals to adults 25 plus.

Rock or Album Oriented Rock consists of a continuous flow of new album releases with comments pertaining to the artists, music, and writers from informed on-air, low key personalities. Music consists of rock, rhythm and blues, country, folk, and jazz. Practically an exclusive FM format, its targeted audience is mostly persons 12 to 34. News and information segments are structured for a young audience. Variations include *Mellow* and *New Music.*

All News is almost exclusively an AM format aimed at the 25 plus targeted audience. It provides instant news in cycles of 12 to 30 minutes presented in depth with remote, eyewitness reports, commentaries, features, and various points of view. The all news pattern is generally maintained 24 hours a day in major markets. Elsewhere, it is used only from 6 A.M. to 8 P.M.

All Talk/Information is programming built around conversations among talk show hosts, guests, and listeners, plus interviews, commentaries, features, in-depth stories, and live sports events.

Black features soul, rhythm and blues, rock, jazz and related music, performed by black artists and presented by black on-air personalities. Directed at blacks of all ages, an emphasis is placed on the 18 to 35 audience. Black oriented news and public affairs are regular features.

Spanish is made up of the music, language, and features that are designed to appeal to Hispanics of all ages.

Ethnic is a format generally used in the top 50 markets. The structure of the format depends on the size of each market and the concentration of persons who speak the languages of each of the ethnic groups therein. Some ethnic stations are directed entirely to one ethnic group while others divide their broadcast day into a series of programs directed to different ethnic groups.

Classical is a format aimed at a highly educated and relatively sophisticated targeted audience of 35 plus. The programming consists of symphony, opera, ballet, chamber, incidental, pop, and jazz offerings. A lighter touch in music is usually presented during the cocktail hour. News and features have a distinctive adult flavor, and the number of commercials is limited.

Nostalgia comprises the popular music from the period of the 1940's through the 1960's plus compatible later releases, excluding rock. Golden Age of Radio entertainment, other historical broadcasts, and light musical selections from later periods are also presented.

News, weather, and sports, depending on the location, are regular features. This format is used mostly in AM radio.

Religion is a collection of religious segments of every conceivable type, manner, and form, including gospel music, bible readings, sermons, discussions, and others. Evangelists, who pay to have their programs broadcast, use this format as fund raising vehicles. The targeted audience for this format is adults 35 plus.

The incomparable Bob and Ray — Robert Brackett Elliott and Raymond Walter Goulding — have delighted radio audiences with brilliant, improvised comedy since 1946. *Courtesy of Goulding-Elliott-Greybar Productions, Inc.*

Chapter Six

The Program Department

Radio is many things to many people, but to most, it is programming and little else. And this should come as no surprise to anyone. As a child, your first exposure to radio probably occurred when you heard sounds coming from a receiver. Later, you discovered that the sounds were programming produced by radio stations and could be changed simply by turning a knob on the receiver. You eventually realized that some of the sounds were more to your liking than others. You began to discriminate among radio stations as your tastes in programming developed based on factors like your age, sex, educational level, occupation, and income.

Although the commercial radio station has been around since the 1920's, few outside the industry understand its workings or the skills required to make one run. Even budding broadcast professionals seldom think of radio in terms other than those that relate to programming. Most careers in radio start at high school, college, or public radio stations which are usually non-profit and not dependent on advertising for operating funds. As a result, the staffs of these stations dedicate most of their efforts to programming.

But a commercial radio station is a business entity. We have seen that the popularity and profit of each station depend upon the extent its targeted audience accepts and approves its programming. Programming is, therefore, a vital part of a station's overall business operation. The program department bears the critical responsibility of creating programming that wins in the competition for audience and advertisers. A radio station is much more than just a disc jockey. But without disc jockeys, music, news, and all of the other elements of modern programming, what is a radio station?

Factors Shaping The Organization
Of The Program Department

The owners and management of a commercial radio station, after considering the factors discussed in Chapter Five, usually select the targeted audience the station shall seek to attract. Thereafter, they adopt a programming policy and format designed to capture and retain that audience. The program department implements that policy and translates it into a format by planning, producing, assembling, and presenting a broadcast schedule.

The program department is the showcase of a radio station. It consists of talented people who work together to create a program schedule and distinctive sound that are consistent with the station's personality or image. It produces the product of a radio station: programming, a service delivered free of charge to all of the people within the station's coverage.

All aspects of programming and the program department are usually the responsibilities of an executive called the *program director* whose position will be discussed below. No two program departments are organized in precisely the same manner. In each situation, the organization of a program department is determined by the following factors:

1. *Size of Market and Station* - As a business entity, a commercial radio station must operate within the financial realities of its environment. The program department of a station in a major market may carry a staff of twenty people and still be considered "slim" compared to its competition. But the entire staff of a small station may consist of twelve people and yet be extravagant when measured by the size of its market.

2. *Program Pattern and Format* - A station operating with an All Music pattern generally requires a smaller, simpler program department than one of comparable size and market which is using a Full Service pattern. By its very nature, a Full Service station operates a more complex program department because of the variety of program elements and on-air personnel used throughout its broadcast schedule. The staff of a program department is also a reflection of its format. For example, a station which operates in an All News format 24 hours a day must have a news director, but will not employ a music director.

3. *Use of Syndicated Program Services and Network Programs* - Program syndicators and networks offer commercial radio stations a wide choice of services which range from entire formats to program elements of all types and lengths, delivered on tape or by satellite. The use of these services affects the organization of a station's program department. For example, a station which uses a Beautiful Music format, purchased from a syndicator or network, might, in certain situations, eliminate the positions of music director and music librarian. Formats like Beautiful Music have been

successfully automated, thereby further influencing program department size and complexity.

4. *Prerogatives of Owners* - Aside from those matters which are within the jurisdiction of the FCC, the ultimate authority within a radio station rests in the hands of its owners. They may dictate the shape of a program department without having to justify their decisions to anyone. Whether based on pure logic, business acumen, or whim, those decisions stand.

A program department of a commercial radio station should be designed to provide: (1) the programming that meets the needs and tastes of the station's targeted audience, and (2) a product saleable to advertisers. Due to the wide variations in the organizational structures of program departments, generalizations about them are of little value. Accordingly, the following discussion concerning a program director and a program department relates to a hypothetical commercial radio station using a Full Service pattern and an Adult Contemporary format in a medium size market.

The Program Director

Almost everyone has an opinion about the "right way" to program a radio station. People who work both inside and outside of the radio industry — station staff members, ad agency personnel, advertisers, and members of the vast radio audience — are all amateur program directors. What differentiates them from the pros is that they would create programming based on their own tastes, designed to please themselves. The professional program director, on the other hand, must produce programming that is based entirely on the preferences of the radio station's targeted audience, without any regard to his personal tastes in programming.

A program director has great responsibilities. He must implement the programming policy and format adopted by the owners and management of the station. He is the leader of the entire programming team and has the responsibility of obtaining the maximum ratings for the station.

While most of the efforts of a program director relate to programming or "creative" activities, he is very much involved in the business end of the station. He, the general manager, and the general sales manager work as a unit to coordinate the programming and sales activities of the station in order to achieve its goals. When these three executives form a communicating, balanced, and functioning team, the result is usually an effectively managed radio station. Where the programming and sales departments are producing good ratings and sales respectively, profits — the business goal of any general manager — will follow.

As a part of the station's management team and the head of the programming department, the program director has many executive and administrative functions. He is, however, primarily responsible for every sound and bit of programming put out over the air by the radio station. Everything that *is* radio to the listener — music, personalities, news, weather, sports — is controlled by the program director. His goal is to produce the best possible and most marketable sound for the station within the budget allowed him by management. The program schedule should be built with only those elements which appeal to the targeted audience. As a result, a program director never takes his eye off the targeted audience. If his judgment is right, the ratings of the station move upward. If he is consistently wrong, he usually moves on.

To be effective, a program director has to make the station's program department a projection of his broadcasting philosophy and style. That philosophy and style must be clearly translated into concise policies and procedures which are communicated to each member of the staff. A written statement of those policies and procedures should be placed in a notebook and made required reading for the entire staff. It should contain specific instructions on the desired procedures to be followed in certain situations. Everyone associated with programming should know precisely what his job is and how it is to be accomplished. This is an area which should not be left to guesswork.

The program director sets broadcast standards for the station, measures all performances and program elements against those standards, and makes adjustments to bring them up where he finds them to be deficient. He constantly listens and analyzes the sound, programs, and formats of competing stations in the market to determine if the opportunity exists to do something better than it is being done or if an unmet need has developed.

The program director is the keeper of the format. As we have seen, music comprises more than 80 percent of all radio programming. In a music format, it is the focus of a great deal of the program director's attention. Each selection of music played by the station should be in harmony with the sound of the format. No music should be used which tends to betray the expectations of the station's loyal listeners who have come to depend on the consistency of its musical policy. For example, a selection by the Rolling Stones would be out of character on a Beautiful Music station.

While the music of a station with a musical format represents the bulk of its programming, the other program elements provide the station with character, identity, and warmth, and are the glue that holds the format together. The program director selects each of these elements with a great deal of care. News, weather, and sports information, and all other features, jingles, and elements must be structured and presented in ways that do no harm to the station's image. The same test applies to commercials. Occasionally, an advertiser must be turned away because its commercials are produced with a sound that is incompatible with the flow of the sound and format of the station. Program elements and commercials that put the station out of character could eventually erode an established audience.

A program director's responsibilities are numerous and diverse. He hires and directs on-air talent and other staff members, makes shift assignments, selects jingles and other audio signatures, deals with program syndicators and networks, stays current with FCC rules and regulations, and oversees the areas of traffic, production, and related areas in programming. In short, the position of program director requires a special individual.

The selection of the right program director is a critical decision for the owners and general manager of a radio station. He is being entrusted with its future. Programming in commercial radio is serious business — one with no room for amateurs equipped only with gleams in their eyes and an abiding love for radio. The job of program director requires a person of excellent personal qualities who is sensitive to the importance of his position. Above all, he must have extensive experience and knowledge of all aspects of radio.

A qualified program director usually starts his career as an unpaid intern (sometimes called a "goffer") at a hometown radio station. He eventually breaks in as an announcer or in some other programming position. Then, he ascends through the ranks of the program departments of various stations, holding different positions. In his travels, he benefits by working with and observing several program directors. His experience in the field of radio is not limited to programming. By starting in smaller stations, he is exposed to many aspects of the business. As a result, he develops a thorough knowledge of all internal and external phases of the radio business and has a wide perspective on broadcasting. As he matures, his awareness and understanding of the world beyond radio is continually expanding.

As does a general manager, a program director draws upon his reservoir of knowledge of radio in order to meet all of the situations which arise daily in the operation of the program department. His ability to recognize and handle these situations is developed through his extensive personal experience in radio. The program director relies heavily on his staff, but his personal responsibility for programming requires that nothing in this area escapes him.

A program director should be an individual of high personal and professional integrity. He must have the respect of his staff, his general manager, his owners, and all segments of the community with which he deals. He must possess and exercise the leadership abilities necessary to motivate his staff, mold it into a winning team, and keep morale high. He constantly must be aware of and concerned about the attitudes and sensitivities of each staff member. Both the program director and each staff member should have the same concept of what that staff member does for the radio station.

The Program Director's Staff

Outstanding programming is the sum of quality production, superior on-air talent, and unique methods of presentation. The program director, as the overseer of all programming activities, can not do it alone. Only a talented and hard working staff can make programming happen.

A radio station usually operates its program department through a series of directors who supervise the music, news, sports, production, promotion, and traffic departments. Some stations, especially those in larger markets, employ directors of operations to oversee all station activities other than in the sales and engineering areas. Others maintain separate news and sports departments whose directors report to their general managers. Each station, depending on its size, market, format, and other factors, has its own particular organizational structure, but the functions of the entire staff of all stations are quite similar.

The following discussion relates to the various directors and staffs which one might expect to find within the program department of our hypothetical commercial radio station using a Full Service pattern and an Adult Contemporary format in a medium size market:

Music Director - Broadcasters know that if a product is good, it will attract listeners. And if listeners are there, advertisers will follow. A station which operates 24 hours a day has 1,440 minutes to fill with programming daily. If it uses a music format, and most commercial radio stations do, the core of its product consists of music that is carefully selected so that it attracts and retains the targeted audience. If it fails to meet this task, the station's audience will soon become its former audience and occupy its time by listening to other stations.

Whether a program director serves as his own music director or appoints a person to that position, the job represents a formidable challenge. He is responsible for fulfilling the music policy of the station. To do so, he must: (1) understand the precise nature of his station's format, including geographical conditions, and other formats present in the market; (2) determine the music and artists the targeted audience wants to hear now; (3) perceive the direction in which the targeted audience's musical tastes are heading, and (4) know the demographic details of the targeted audience and the manner in which they are changing.

One begins to comprehend the monumental task of a music director when he considers the broad spectrum of musical preferences which exist. Music is a trendy business which runs in cycles. Within any musical category, a sound gets hot and stays on top for a while.

Eventually, yesterday's hot sound cools down. A small portion of that sound becomes a part of the ever expanding American musical heritage, but the bulk of the once hot sound then descends into oblivion.

A music director must be tuned in to the trends that develop within his format and move quickly with them. His ability to identify the trends needs to be sharp, but he must also avoid moving too quickly and causing a radical change in his product, thereby putting the station out of character in the judgment of the targeted audience. At the same time, he does not wish to react too slowly and be left at the starting gate by competing stations programming the same format.

It is never an accident when a music director is "right" in executing the music policy of his station. He has to do his homework. The play list of a radio station is the result of intensive analyses of many bits of information about hits and trends which are drawn from a number of sources. Commercial surveys, publications, and record companies provide a great deal of this data. Many music directors do their own research through surveys and other means. Some gauge new releases by previewing them with test audiences and measuring their reactions to them before the tunes are broadcast. Others make their programming decisions based on their own instincts, use the new releases on the air, and measure the reactions of their audiences by sophisticated sampling procedures, interviews, questionnaires, formulae for statistical analysis with computer programs, and a myriad of other techniques and complex procedures. Indeed, programming is serious business.

Prior to 1960, certain radio station employees accepted cash and other items from record manufacturers and distributors to play certain releases over the air. These "play for pay" schemes are called *payola* and *plugola*. The FCC adopted strict rules prohibiting these practices, and Congress enacted legislation under which both the giver and the receiver in a payola deal are subject to criminal prosecution.

The staff available to and used by a music director varies from station to station. It is composed of musical librarians, researchers, and clerical people who assist him in charting the direction of the format and maintaining the station's storehouse of musical programming. The efforts of the music director and his staff are also augmented by independent consultants who specialize in programming.

News Director - The strength of a radio station's news department depends upon the capabilities of the station's news director who should be experienced in both journalism and broadcasting. His job begins with the recruiting of a staff whose members are competent and committed to the principles of good journalism. He is also responsible for adopting and enforcing a news policy that requires each newsperson to report accurately, objectively, and clearly. Due to its great mobility — reporters need only a telephone, not the complex equipment of television — radio should be first to break the story of a newsworthy event. But the need to be first should not take priority over the station's primary responsibility — that of being accurate.

The quality of broadcast journalism depends on the quality of its journalists and the freedom they have to do their jobs. Over half of all Americans depend on radio for their daily news. They rely on the competence and integrity of radio news people. There is no room for sloppy, unsubstantiated reporting. The credibility of a radio station must be earned and can not be taken for granted.

No matter what the format or targeted audience of a station may be, it must live by the principles of good journalism. The form, length, and placement of newscasts, however, are affected by programming considerations. News, commercials, and all elements of the broadcast schedule are programming, and each element must complement the entire format. The in-depth approach to news that would be suitable for a station with an All Talk format would not work in a Beautiful Music format.

Radio news consists of reports of events or opinions which have meaning to a large number of listeners. The most important news stories are those reports which have the greatest meaning to the greatest number of people. The content of a newscast is generated by the work of full-time staff reporters and stringers, various wire services (such as the Associated Press), and regional and national networks.

The news director oversees the entire news operation. He monitors the performance of his staff, all of the major news stories, and the coverage afforded those stories by competing radio stations, television outlets, and newspapers. He concerns himself with the quality of the delivery of the news and works with the program director to insure that newscasts fit within the selected format. He also handles administrative matters such as making news assignments and setting up broadcast schedules. He represents the station at many public functions and maintains lines of communication with persons in all levels of government, education, health, and other areas that affect the public.

The staff of a large news department usually consists of the news director, newspersons, and sometimes a few clerical assistants who are, among other things, responsible for retaining written and recorded news stories. The full-time staff is frequently augmented by stringers.

Sports Director - Another facet of radio news is sports programming. Most stations place all sports under the supervision of the news director who also serves as sports director. Once again, bear in mind that the organizational structures of radio stations vary. A station that places a great deal of emphasis on sports will engage a sports director to operate a separate sports department.

Sports shows are usually considered news programming. They should be done with the same journalistic approach, with the emphasis being placed on accuracy. While the practice of focusing sports reporting on the hometown team has not only become acceptable, it is usually essential. The slanting of sports coverage in favor of the locals is unacceptable in the view of most sports journalists — although most would concede the pressures to "puff" frequently result in just that.

Each major league team usually retains the ownership of the play-by-play broadcasts of its games. It buys a block of time from a station for each game to be broadcast for which it pays a fixed fee and provides the station with availabilities within the game broadcasts. Under this type of arrangement, the announcers are usually employees of the team. An FCC order requires that where the announcers are hired and/or paid by anyone other than the radio station, a disclaimer to that effect must be announced during the broadcast of each game.

Since sports fans are very knowledgeable about their favorite types of competition, a sports director must be selective in assigning persons to do radio sports and play-by-play reporting. In a matter of seconds, the sports audience knows if the announcer is a professional or is simply winging it. A mispronounced name, an incorrectly quoted rule, or any sign of deficiency results in a loss of the audience's faith in the announcer's credibility. You can't fool a true sports fan.

Sports programming is big business on radio. Broadcasts of local, state, and national events fit neatly into the program schedules of many stations which use All Talk and other information formats. Baseball, hockey, basketball, and football games are usually played in non-drive time periods, and they attract loyal and intelligent followings. For locally originated amateur sports, a station or the team usually brings in specialists or assigns a qualified staffer to call a game. Regional and national network sports broadcasts are usually called by prominent broadcasters, some of whom are former athletes. Sports programming requires other specialists such as statisticians and persons with the special engineering expertise required to set up remote broadcasts from ballparks, arenas, and other competition sites.

Knowledgeable announcers recently have been successful in attracting sizeable audiences with talk shows devoted entirely to sports. Well known sports figures, from the comfort of their own homes, are able to participate in these shows by telephone.

Production Director - If he is good, the production director of a radio station is a modern day wizard. By use of some very modest tools — the spoken word, sound effects, recorded music, and some electronic devices (echo chamber, etc.) — he is able to create illusions by which he shares ideas, emotions, and experiences with the listener. His productions play against the human mind to produce fantasies through sound. The pounding surf, crickets chirping at night, 100,000 cheering fans at the Super Bowl — all on tape and happening in the imagination of the listener.

The wizardry of the production director and his staff is used today in radio mostly in the creation of commercial announcements, public service spots, and promotional material for the station. The production people are usually assigned a studio which has been specially equipped to assist them in creating their unique brand of magic. The special equipment consists of a board or mixer which allows all types of sound from many sources (microphone, tape, record, etc.) to be combined in the proper audio levels to produce the desired effects. A 30 second commercial or public service announcement may take hours to produce, but if the product is "a great spot," it is all worth it.

Production activities require a great deal of cooperation among the various radio station employees. In the creation of commercials, salespersons and advertising agency people often work with the production staff in order to achieve the results promised to advertisers. A station may pick up and retain certain business because of its superior production capabilities.

The production director is responsible for seeing that no spot, public service announcement, or promotional matter conflicts with the station's image as it is perceived by the targeted audience. Since the production people play an important role in creating the on-air matter that produces the image of the radio station itself, they must be dedicated to maintaining that image at all times. As an example, the audio signatures and themes of a station are created to achieve specific results. The sounds which introduce various features are selected to serve as bridges between the different programming elements, and, at the same time, keep the station's image intact. If a program director decided to set off newscasts within a Beautiful Music format by audio signatures, those employed should be dignified and in harmony with the station image but, nevertheless, sufficiently different from the regular sound so as to direct the listener's attention to the news.

The production director's staff usually consists of a copywriter and specialists who operate the production studio, edit and file tape recordings, and devise sound effects of all sorts. The production studio contains a large number of sound source equipment such as turntables, cartridge machines, and reel to reel tapes.

Promotion Director - The goal of the promotion director is identical to that of the program director — to build and maintain a large targeted audience that is faithful to the radio station and loyal to its on-air personalities. The promotion director just uses different tools to accomplish the goal.

Radio promotion covers two general areas — *audience* promotion and *sales* promotion. Sales promotion is discussed in Chapter Eight. Audience promotion is accomplished by using program segments broadcast over the station (on-air promotion) and by promotion techniques that use all other forms of media (off-air promotion).

As is the case with all other activities under the jurisdiction of the program director, all promotion must be created with the targeted audience in mind. The demographics of the targeted audience, the type of the station, and its general sound are all factors to be considered when establishing promotional goals. Promotion must not be a happenstance or a casual activity. It requires a carefully structured plan with a defined goal. This goal may be long or short term. All promotion goals ultimately are determined by the program director and executed by the promotion director and his staff.

On-air promotion is a radio station selling itself by radio. It is accomplished by carefully created jingles, identification tags, creative promotional announcements about programs and personalities featured by the station, contests, and many other devices — all hooks which state simply, "try us — you'll like us." Great promotional material on the air is an inducement for the listener to stay tuned for more great programming. If they hear it and like it, the targeted audience will stay put.

Off-air promotion is actually a misnomer. Many stations use other radio and television stations as part of their promotional activities. It is common for a beautiful music station to purchase commercial time on all news or daytime stations whose formats are less likely to retain all of their own listeners for the entire broadcast day. Annually, radio station promotion is one of the best revenue producers for local television stations. Off-air promotion may, therefore, be on the air, but not on the air of the station being promoted.

Off-air promotion is more expensive than on-air efforts, but it is an essential part of the total promotional scheme of a radio station. It is particularly critical in the battle to enlarge the station's actual audience because it reaches out and touches individuals in the targeted audience who are not current listeners of the station, but should be. A person is incapable of remembering that which he never knew. Off-air promotion seeks to provide a non-listener with something to remember when he tunes in his radio.

The list of off-air vehicles is practically endless. At the present time, stations use other radio stations, television, newspapers, magazines, billboards, signs on buses and taxis, store windows, bumper stickers, station banners, tee shirts, and everything else including skywriters. Very often, on-air personalities of the station are used to make personal appearances at many functions including charitable activities. Stations also sponsor concerts and other activities that are complementary with their images and formats.

The promotion director generally has a clerical staff and publicity assistant. Some stations engage advertising agencies and public relations firms to assist to their promotional activities.

Traffic Manager - Time is money to the radio broadcaster. Any income lost due to availabilities not sold or commercials sold by not properly run is gone forever. The traffic department is a bridge between the programming and sales departments. It is the heart of a radio station's operation. Its objectives are to eliminate errors, prevent duplication, and make sure that all departments of the station know what is and is not scheduled for broadcast. Without a properly functioning traffic department, chaos would exist at most commercial radio stations.

The traffic manager has the responsibility of preparing the daily logs of all of the station's programming using information provided by the program, sales, and engineering departments, its national sales representative, and, where applicable, its network. Each program element, no matter what its source, broadcast over the air must be cleared through the traffic manager who creates and distributes the paper work to all station personnel who need to know what is being broadcast and when. The traffic manager also prepares sheets which advise sales personnel about the time periods for commercials which are yet unsold. He also handles a substantial amount of detail work and is constantly under the pressure of meeting daily deadlines.

Traffic work used to be tedious manual record keeping. Though the development of sophisticated business systems and computers has eased the burdens on traffic personnel, the successful traffic manager still must be familiar with the entire program schedule and each of its elements. He must be an accurate individual with an orderly mind who works well under fire. His staff comprises technicians and clerical personnel who must have a thorough understanding of the details and the importance of their jobs.

Jerry Bishop, prominent West Coast freelance announcer and morning man, at work in the Los Angeles area.

Chapter Seven

Radio Performers

Pilot of the airwaves,
Here is my request.
You don't have to play it,
But I hope you'll do your best.
I've been listening to your show
on the radio,
And you seem like a friend to me. *

The sounds of radio are capable of weaving illusions, creating fantasies, and producing just about every character and situation within the
scope of a listener's imagination. This virtually limitless dimension of
radio applies to every aspect of programming. Radio emancipates the
listener's mind, allowing it to roam freely beyond those limits imposed
by the people and things he actually sees. It projects the listener into a
world created within his own mind through the talents of radio artists.

Radio reaches people through words, music, and sounds. Consider
how easy it is to enjoy radio programming. All one has to do is listen.
Whether a format provides a musical background for the listener's
activities or involves him directly in foreground programming, such as
in the case of talk shows, he is able to do whatever else he wishes
because radio listening requires no visual or manual activity — his eyes
and hands are free. No other medium supported by advertising dollars
can make that statement. If you don't believe that, try watching television or reading a newspaper next time you drive to work.

Commercial radio is everywhere and offers something for everyone.
More than 8,000 stations provide programming that is received by

millions of listeners every day. In the United States alone, over 550 million radios in working order are located in residences, businesses, vehicles, and everywhere else people are found. Geographic, demographic, and programming diversities create great competition for listeners and advertisers among the stations in each market, especially those using similar formats. Each seeks to achieve an edge with its targeted audience.

Modern radio is a highly personal medium. Gone are the days when rating services estimated the number of "households listening." Today, targeted audiences consist of people, not houses. No matter how great the total audience of a particular radio station may be at any time, its programming is created for and directed to one person — a hypothetical composite listener who personifies the members of its targeted audience during a particular day-part.

Radio deals with ideas and events on a person-to-person basis. A station *communicates* with its audience through various programming elements, but it *speaks* to each listener with a human voice — that of the performer. Strong on-air performers give a station an edge over competitors by establishing strong personal relationships with its listeners and promoting their friendship, loyalty, and involvement. Music and other features are all needed to attract and retain a targeted audience, but the performer is radio's most important programming element. The magnetism of a strong radio personality is incomparable.

Radio provides entertainment, information, and companionship for its listeners. Each of us has his own particular reasons for tuning in a specific station at any given time. Whether it is the type of music, the sports coverage, or the frequent traffic and weather checks, something in that station's programming causes each of its listeners to choose it over all of the other offerings available across the dial. On-air performers top the list of attractions that draw and retain listeners. Often, a particular performer *is* the radio station to its audience.

Listeners are less than scientific when bestowing their favors on a radio performer. They are not interested at all in programming philosophies, the structure of the program department, or the workings of the radio station. They have found a guy on the radio who talks to them, plays their kind of music, and is a friend. If the performer continues to treat his audience right, he retains its attention — until someone better comes along. As time passes, the performer becomes a listening habit of his audience. Thereafter, its loyalty to him is hard to shake.

The only programming element capable of giving a radio station warm and human qualities is the on-air performer, be he disc jockey, straight announcer, talk show host, newscaster, commercial pitchman, or actor. The tone, mood, and pace of his voice and words meld all of the carefully crafted programming elements of a format into a distinctive sound. Even where the personalities of performers have intentionally been deemphasized, as is the case in the Good Music formats heard mostly on FM, the style and bearing of each such performer shape a station's sound and create its desired ambiance.

Good on-air performers are *made*, not born. Each usually comes to radio with a degree of natural talent, but his development as a professional requires much more. The performer is an artist who must constantly seek to grow and emulate the best in the field. He must work hard together with his program director in order to achieve success for himself and the radio station. With the programming "big picture" constantly in mind, the program director should guide each performer so that his talents and efforts work well and naturally within the station's format.

The successful execution of a station's format requires a concerted effort by each member of the program department. An on-air performer is an important player on this team. Maintaining the station's personality and tying all of the program elements into the format are his chief responsibilities. The status and functions of a radio performer and an airline pilot are analogous. Both are literally "up front" and appear to be in control of their environments — the radio station and the airliner. But without the support of their respective teams, neither would get off the ground.

Images, Characters, and Personalities Through Voices and Words

Every performer creates his image, character, or personality on the air by what he says and how he says it. Facial expressions, gestures, and body movements are meaningless in radio communications. By allowing his audience to hear just those things which develop the image, character, or personality he wishes to create, the performer controls the way it perceives him.

A radio performer, working with the station's program director, should determine the type of character he will portray on the air and the manner in which it shall be done. As a professional, he has developed a particular style and delivery, but these will be subordinated if necessary to satisfy the needs of the station. His creative efforts should complement the format of the station. A disc jockey, for example, is ordinarily hired by a station because his personality, style, and delivery fit its format. Prior to his first show, the "jock" and his program director should agree on the type of character he will portray to best serve the station — regardless of the approaches he used at previous stations. Will he be cool or mellow, abrasive or bright, funny or just plain nasty? Once the performer determines the nature of his character, he and the rest of the programming team try to bring it to life. An established personality is usually exempt from the process described above. He is ordinarily hired because management hopes his name, reputation, and unique style will add sparkle to the station's image. In other situations, due to market, format, and management preferences, this process is not used.

Any performer must understand his audience in order to please it. An actor in a theater, a rock group in concert, and a politician at a podium actually see, hear, and feel their audiences. They know soon enough if they are reaching them. But a radio performer must also visualize his audience — so how does he see, hear, and feel it? A morning man at a 50 kW radio station in a major market may reach more than a quarter of a million listeners each day. If he could see that mass of humanity at one time, he would probably be awestruck and unable to speak. The radio performer seldom thinks of his audience as being one large mass of people. Rather, he visualizes it as being one person — that hypothetical composite listener with the characteristics of the station's targeted audience.

While a radio performer does not actually see his audience, he hears from it in many ways. He senses the results of his efforts on the air through mail and telephone calls from listeners and direct contact with them at personal appearances. But a performer really "hears" from his audience through ratings. In those formats which rely on strong performers, good ratings are usually the result of both the efforts of an on-air performer and the correct blend of programming elements in the right format aimed at a receptive targeted audience. While a performer is but one of those programming elements, his contributions to those ratings are measurable by surveys and other methods.

A performer who establishes rapport with his listeners through his personality and style becomes "a member of the family" as the years roll on. However, the relationship between performer and audience is not indestructible. A performer who maintains his routine and fails to adapt to the times runs the risk of boring his audience. On the other hand, sudden changes in his routine may put him out of character and jolt his listeners, driving them to other performers and stations. To strike a balance between these extremes, a performer must possess great sensitivity and a thorough understanding of his audience. He may not see his listeners, but he must know who they are, where they are, and what they want to hear.

Radio Performers and Broadcast Roles

Anyone who takes the microphone at a radio station is an actor. Whether creating a dramatic or comedic character or filling an established radio role, the on-air performer is playing a part. Even one who plays *himself* on the air is an actor and should consider how he wants his audience to perceive him. He controls, to some extent, the way he is perceived by what he says and how he says it. For example, if a business leader were appointed the chairman of a local fund raising charity for the benefit of needy children — a very serious subject, he should strive to sound the part on the air and avoid the use of crude, frivolous banter during an interview. The credibility of both the chairman and the charity he seeks to serve are at stake.

The radio performer is a pure actor when he creates a dramatic or comedic character. Performers who possess acting ability are used by a radio station in the production of commercials, promotional material, and other elements. In addition, radio actors are, to a limited extent, being used again on regularly scheduled network dramatic shows. Acting is an art which requires study, understanding, and experience. But there are no shortcuts. One must act in order to learn how to act. To act effectively in radio, a performer should possess the abilities to analyze the character he is called upon to create and to exercise the voice control required to create it. Whatever the vehicle, a radio actor must determine the function of his character within the context of the entire work and understand its relationship to the other characters. He then establishes the mood, pace, and overall impact of the character. The listener is treated as if he were blind. Microphone techniques and sound effects assist the actor, but his voice and words project a character into the mind of the listener. To do so, a radio actor must have control of his voice, good tonal and emotional ranges, and a sense of timing.

Since the 60's, the established radio roles — announcers, newscasters, disc jockeys, talk show hosts, sportscasters, weather reporters, and the like — have undergone some changes due to the creation and modification of new formats and programming concepts. But most listeners expect these roles to be played in essentially traditional ways. For example, a newscaster usually reads reports on the air with a serious delivery and tone. Although some newscasts end with a humorous story, the credibility of a newscaster would suffer greatly if his entire report were performed in a giddy, unconcerned fashion. In the creation of any of these established roles, a performer must find a middle ground between the manner in which the role is usually performed (what the audience expects to hear) and his own style and delivery.

The most intense competition in radio occurs among stations which feature similar music formats and attempt to attract the same targeted audience. Since most of their programming consists of play lists of musical selections local surveys indicate the targeted audience wants to hear, the stations in the chase feature essentially the same artists and recordings. To set itself apart from the rest of the pack, each station attempts to create the most pleasing overall image by using various programming elements. The station's on-air performers are usually the most important elements in this image making process. As a result, each performer should be the personification of the image management wants the station to have in the market. As we have seen, the

professional should know what he is supposed to do and how he is
going to do it before he actually goes on the air.

A field in which change is a way of life, modern radio requires the
services of an array of on-air performers. No two stations or markets are
identical. The functions of the performers who play established roles
differ from station to station. The following is a general discussion of
the various roles and some of their basic functions and requirements.

Staff Announcers. Long before the world heard of disc jockeys, talk
show hosts, newscasters, and traffic reporters, the announcer was the
voice of the infant radio industry. The first announcers were engineers.
They ran the stations, spoke on the air, and urged listeners to let them
know when and where the stations were being received. As the radio
industry developed, engineering and performing became separate, specialized skills. On-air performers called *staff announcers* handled a
great deal of the performing for radio stations and networks. To the
radio audience, the announcer was the station or network. Listeners
related to him and gave little thought to any other aspect of the station
or network to which they were tuned. He was called upon to handle all
speaking related assignments. He introduced shows, announced classical and popular musical selections, read commercials and public
service messages, conducted interviews, delivered news, weather, and
sports reports, and performed many other, on-air assignments. Most
of his efforts were scripted, but he had to be ready to extemporize or ad
lib at any time.

While some staff announcers work for a few established radio networks and some major market full service stations, the position is
rapidly becoming a thing of the past. The present day on-air performer
is much more of a specialist. His primary responsibilities at a station
usually are limited to a specific role, such as disc jockey. Whether he
serves a station in other capacities depends on the size of the station.
On-air personnel of larger stations generally have but one job. In
smaller operations, they may have a number of responsibilities both on
and off the air. For example, a sportscaster may write and perform
commercial and promotional copy before and after his airshift. For the
balance of this chapter, the term "announcer" means anyone who does
on-air performing in any role.

Today's radio listeners are very discerning. They have many stations
and formats from which to choose, and their loyalties change quickly.
As a result, each program director has to define his station's targeted
audience closely. An announcer must adjust his approach to suit that
targeted audience. He should project a positive attitude, sound natural, execute the policies and procedures of the station, and conform to
FCC regulations. He also ought to be familiar with the station's
technical equipment — the tools of the trade. Various tasks which
engineers used to perform manually are now done by announcers by

pushing buttons while they are on the air. An announcer should have sufficient technical experience and ability to improvise if unexpected things happen, as they always seem to do in radio.

The quality of an announcer's voice is important to his career as a performer, but it is not as critical as it used to be. At one time, only men with deep, resonant voices and excellent elocution were considered for positions in announcing. Things have changed considerably. Women announcers are finally commonplace in broadcasting. An audience is more concerned about what an announcer has to say rather than how he says it. Speech localisms, once taboo in radio, are now acceptable. Listeners, however, show little patience for inept announcing. Try to recall your own reaction the last time you heard a radio performer mispronounce a familiar name. The listener expects the message to be delivered with exact pronounciation and proper grammar by a pleasant voice with warm, positive mannerisms.

Proficiency in announcing is achieved, as it is in any other professional undertaking, by a thorough study of the field, guidance by knowledgeable supervisors, and plenty of practical experience. Whether gained through working at a high school or college radio station, interning at a commercial or public station, or studying at a qualified school of broadcasting that provides a well-structured curriculum and simulated broadcasting conditions, any experience is very helpful in landing that first job in radio as a performer. Aside from learning how to do the job, the young announcer must become familiar with FCC rules and regulations. For example, no one should go on the air without a thorough knowledge of the "when, where, and how" of a legal station identification.

Hosts of Musical Shows and Formats. The formats used by a radio station dictate the types of on-air performers it needs. Some stations operate with one format continuously while other stations employ two or more formats during each 24 hour period. For example, it is common for a full service station to use an Adult Contemporary format from 6 A.M. to 8 P.M. and switch to All Talk from 8 P.M. to 6 A.M.

Music dominates the formats used in commercial radio, and, as a result, the largest category of on-air performers consists of hosts or anchormen who conduct musical programs. The *disc jockey*, or D.J., is probably America's most familiar host. He made his debut in radio in the 1950's when the networks' domination of the radio industry was diminishing, and they were providing less programming to their affiliates. At the same time, legal prohibitions against the use of phonograph recordings on the air were set aside. With a great deal of air time to fill locally, many station owners turned to the disc jockey and his "stack of platters" as a major source of programming, and the D.J. has since become a staple of American radio.

The disc jockey is one who conducts a radio program of recorded rock, popular, or contemporary music. But he is much more. He is, first and foremost, the listener's buddy, companion, and entertainer. He tries to be that nice guy with whom the listener wants to spend some time. His show contains a rapid succession of hit recordings and program elements which could easily overwhelm the listener. But the D.J.'s personality, humor, and ability to keep the show moving make the whole package palatable to his audience.

The disc jockey is a music specialist. He is required to know each current music survey cold, the status of every recording, and the history and current activities of the musical groups featured on his show. He lives in a world of new releases, live concerts, and whatever else is happening in the particular realm of his audience. He must possess the same basic professional qualities that are required of all announcers plus a certain intangible something which produces a type of communion with his audience. The disc jockey employs a keen sense of humor attuned to his listeners, a finely honed sense of timing, and the ability to use the inflection, the pause, and a great deal of sparkle to produce a show in which an audience can participate. He also must be the consummate salesperson who lends credibility to each commercial he reads.

The ability of a disc jockey to integrate his patter, music, commercial copy, information services, and other programming elements, and make sense out of it all, is called style. And a disc jockey must work hard to produce his own style. It requires many hours in front of the microphone. Actual show business experience is also very helpful because he often is called upon to serve as master of ceremonies at live concerts and other events. Working a stadium full of fans is considerably different than speaking into a microphone in a studio and visualizing an audience of one listener.

The radio host who enjoys the greatest longevity is the *morning man.* Some have been with stations for more than a quarter of a century. The morning man is the ultimate listening habit — the early bird who owns the airwaves between 5 A.M. and 10 A.M. Their styles vary greatly. Some bubble with exhuberance while others sound as if they also just got out of bed. No matter what his style or the music format in use at his station, the morning man's show has to contain certain programming elements. News, weather, sports, traffic data, school closings, ski reports, high and low tide schedules, and other information must be included if important to the targeted audience and relevant in the market.

As we have seen, no matter what format in which he works, a morning man plays the role of a good friend who doles out a great deal of useful information in a calm way for the benefit of his audience at a frantic time of the workday. The kind of music format does, however, affect the approach taken by other types of on-air hosts. An announcer who serves as a host within a format that features clusters of musical selections, such as Beautiful Music and Easy Rock, seeks to be as

Don Imus, the main morning man in the Big Apple. *Courtesy of NBC Radio Division.*

unobtrusive as possible so that he does not interfere with the relaxed ambiance the programming formula is designed to achieve.

Hosts of Classical and Jazz formats deal with audiences that are generally knowledgeable and caring about the music, composers, and performers that are featured. In order to satisfy these audiences, each host must have a thorough education and background in his particular field. He also should exhibit an abiding respect for the music. These listeners take an intellectual approach to their music and expect the same from such a host. Some hosts who work Album Oriented Rock and other formats deal with their roles similarly.

The preceding is not intended as a catalogue of the numerous approaches taken by music hosts in radio today. It is, however, designed to demonstrate that nothing in radio programming should happen by accident. Each on-air element — including the role to be played by a music host — requires thinking, planning, and analysis by the program director.

Newscasters. When Americans want to know what's happening, they turn to radio. Its coverage of fast breaking news events is virtually instantaneous. The radio *newsman* or *newscaster* is able to convey a story to millions as it occurs. The development of the communications satellite system has made live global coverage a reality. Each local radio station, no matter what its format, is able to mobilize its staff and convert its operation from its usual pattern or format into a news center should a major event require immediate, comprehensive coverage.

The format employed by each station determines the amount and depth of regularly scheduled news coverage. Some carry little or no news programming while many use an All News format. In the discussion that follows, the news coverage referred to consists of more than headlines and "newsman" or "newscaster" means one who finds, writes, and reports the news on the air as opposed to an announcer who merely reads news copy prepared by others.

A radio newscaster must be informed before he is able to inform others. He must understand society and know about people. He needs both an academic education and "real world" experience to cope with the mass and diversity of information with which he deals. He faces a steady stream of complex situations which must be explained to his audience within short periods of time. He usually has to cover international, national, regional, local, sports, and weather items on the air within one to three minutes.

The first responsibility of a newsman is to be a good journalist. He should get his stories fast and straight, make them understandable, and always be fair. Time constraints in radio usually prohibit lengthy discussions by newsmen of the larger questions the stories raise, but there is never an excuse for sloppy, biased reporting.

The essence of radio journalism is the ability to communicate by sound. As a radio performer, a newscaster must master the tools of his trade, and the primary one is the human voice. He should concentrate on communicating to the listener rather than talking down to him. His delivery and style should never create an obstacle between the news and his listeners. Rather, his voice should be smooth and devoid of distracting mannerisms. His delivery and style ought to be professional, but he must avoid stuffiness. Listeners want to be informed, not lectured. Pace, timing, and concern create an aura of credibility about the newscaster.

A great voice and polished style do not make a complete radio newscaster. The professional must master the English language, develop writing skills adopted for the medium, and be able to utilize all of the technical tools such as the wire services, tape recorders, and related items. Except in large radio news operations in major markets or in All News formats, the radio newscaster does it all by himself. Experience as a reporter with a high school or college radio station or newspaper, or as an intern with any of the news media is helpful to an individual seeking a career in radio news.

Sportscasters. Most commercial radio stations in the United States include some sports coverage in their daily programming. The amount carried is determined by each station's format, targeted audience, and other factors. The subject of sports is covered in two distinct ways by radio. First, it is treated on most stations as a specialized type of news presented either as part of regular newscasts or in separate sportscasts. These reports consist of scores, analysis, features, and interviews. A *sportscaster*, the host who does this type of reporting, should be generally familiar with sports. He also must be a competent announcer — capable of presenting sports news with a certain degree of excitement and enthusiasm which demonstrates his involvement in sports.

Play-by-play coverage of live events is the other type of sports programming. These broadcasts, done with the aura of news coverage of an event, are actually more properly described as entertainment programming. As mentioned earlier, when local announcers began to focus on the home team during live coverage and the teams were given a say in hiring the on-air performers, it became somewhat difficult to classify this coverage as "news."

The play-by-play sportscaster must know his business. Through hard work and experience, he needs to develop instant recall of facts relating to players, rules, teams, leagues, history, folklore, and every other aspect of the sport being covered. The ability to ad lib, fill, and maintain a high level of interest and enthusiasm is mandatory. Since no area of broadcasting is more susceptible to hackneyed statements than sports, the sportscaster should strive to be unique, fresh, and bright.

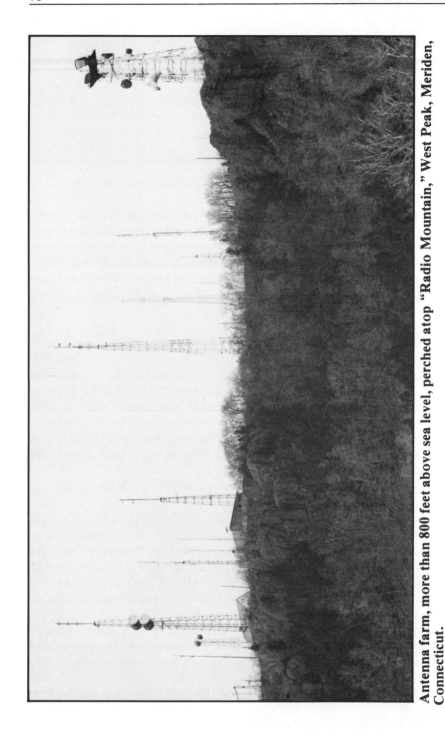

Antenna farm, more than 800 feet above sea level, perched atop "Radio Mountain," West Peak, Meriden, Connecticut.

No matter what type of sports coverage is involved, the sportscaster faces radio's most difficult listener — the sports fan. He is involved and opinionated. The sportscaster must *earn* respect from his listener through consistent and accurate reporting, delivered with a distinctive approach.

The best experience for a sportscaster consists of involvement in all phases of sports. His actual participation in sports adds depth to his capacity to cover an event. Former professional athletes have used their playing experience to great advantage in this area. But that is not enough. The ability to communicate is the primary reason for the success of any on-air performer.

Talk Show Hosts. A *talk show host* should be a professional devil's advocate. He also must be a good listener, a conversationalist, and a well informed person. While constantly reminding his audience that his questions do not necessarily reflect his opinions, he must take positions and propose hypothetical situations that keep the show moving. Carefully selected subject matter for a given talk show keeps the action topical and interesting to the audience. Discussion categories which are of little or no interest to the general public cause a great drop off in the size of the audience.

Today, talk show hosts with specific professional credentials in particular areas are gaining popularity. Lawyers, doctors, psychologists, clergymen, and others have been serving as hosts on regularly scheduled talk shows. Also, talk shows devoted to specific subjects such as religion and sports have come into vogue.

The successful talk show host never actually succeeds in completely masking his own opinions. Tolerance for the opinions of others is the key to his success. By recognizing that any given story has more than one side, the talk show host earns the respect of his listeners even though they might not share his views. Listeners are more concerned with his manners than with his opinions. The courteous and calm handling of a boisterous caller garners a great deal of admiration for the host. Rude, sarcastic, and bad tempered responses generally offend audiences, but some hosts attract large audiences simply by being obnoxious. In order to be an interesting talk show host, one must be interested. An obviously bored individual is not capable of sustaining audience participation in a talk show for any length of time. Guests who appear at the studio or participate by telephone add diversity to talk shows. A broad general background and a cool head are standard equipment for talk show hosts. The careful screening of callers and a taped delay keep things moving.

Specialists. Modern radio requires the services of many *specialists* who provide a great deal of information packaged in short shows. Airborne traffic reporters, weathermen, business analysts, and others supply important data on a daily basis. Each specialist need not be a superb announcer, but must have sufficient voice and delivery quality so that the listener understands the programming with ease.

A specialist's work must be credible. The audience should believe that he knows his stuff. His education, experience, and publications in his field should be promoted by the station. It is essential, however, that the specialist does not sound like a robot. The judicious use of humor never hurts — even when delivering the closing stock market prices.

NASA launches Delta 159 with RCA SATCOM E satellite on board from Kennedy Space Center, Florida on January 15, 1982. *Courtesy of National Aeronautics and Space Agency and RCA.*

Chapter Eight

Radio Sales

Creative programming, with its excitement, immediacy, and on-air performers, is the product that attracts an audience to a commercial radio station. Modern broadcast engineering, discussed in Chapter Nine, provides each station with a dynamic delivery system that brings that product to its audience. As indispensable as both programming and engineering are to each station, without sales, it can not survive. A commercial radio station is an enterprise that depends upon the successful marketing of its product for revenue. It competes for that revenue in the world of advertising.

Advertising and Advertising Agencies

Advertising is a method of selling. It consists of a number of actions designed to attract the attention of the general public to a product, service, or idea. Advertising is also the business of preparing and distributing advertisements. Advertisers pay for advertisements that inform prospective customers about the benefits of whatever they are selling for the purpose of inducing them to buy. Everyone advertises —businesses, governments, colleges, and even radio stations.

Advertisements are carried to people by vehicles called *media.* *Webster's New Collegiate Dictionary* defines a medium as

> "......a means of effecting or conveying something: as (1): a substance regarded as the means of transmission of a force or effect (2): a surrounding or enveloping substance b pl usu media (1): a channel of communication (2): a publication or broadcast that carries advertising (3): a mode of artistic expression or communication......"*

The most commonly used media are radio, television, newspapers, magazines, direct mail, billboards, and bus posters. When evaluating

* "By permission. From Webster's Collegiate Dictionary 1981 by G. & C. Merriam Co., publishers of the Merriam-Webster Dictionaries."

the effectiveness of a particular medium for their products and services, advertisers consider its targeted audience, circulation, and cost among other factors. The use by an advertiser of two or more media in one advertising plan is called a *mixed media campaign.*

Before making any decisions about the media it should use, an advertiser has to determine how it wants to be perceived and what marketing goals it seeks to achieve through an ad campaign. It also must understand its current markets, identify new markets to be targeted, and adopt an effective advertising plan. Since misdirected advertising is a waste of money, such complex decisions should not be made by amateurs through guesswork.

While some large companies maintain their own advertising departments, most businesses retain advertising agencies to create and place their advertising. Agencies bring together experts from many fields, including research, merchandising, copywriting, commercial art, sales, and media selection. Working as a team, they plan, create, and place advertising for each client of the agency. National, regional, and local advertising agencies come in all sizes and have many specialties. For example, some agencies work exclusively in one field, such as manufacturing, banking, or insurance. Most, however, handle a wide variety of clients.

An *account executive* of an agency oversees the advertising plans and campaigns of his clients. He deals directly with each client and coordinates the efforts of the agency's departments on its behalf.

Most income earned by an agency is from commissions paid by the advertising media. An agency charges its client for the total amount it is billed by the medium. When the client pays, a fee equal to 15 percent of the total amount is retained by the agency, and the medium accepts 85 percent of its bill in full payment. This has been standard procedure in the industry, but other compensation arrangements are now being used. Agencies also earn income for research, surveys, and special projects done for clients. They are usually paid on an hourly basis.

Advertisers need answers to some basic questions before they adopt advertising plans. The advertiser should have realistic marketing goals, a definite budget, and an ad copy theme that works. As a result, an advertising agency must become familiar with each client's business through an objective analysis of its entire operation. The agency's staff is then able to analyze market data and use its creative expertise to devise and recommend an effective plan.

A business which sells on the national level usually works with an agency throughout the entire decision making process. It advises the advertiser about the merits of various media as they relate to its particular products or services. It does the research, analyzes the data, produces the commercials or print advertisements, selects the appropriate markets in which the advertising is placed, and chooses the media within those markets. On the local level, an agency does many of the same things for its clients, but on a smaller scale. Some local advertisers do not use agencies and deal directly with the media.

Radio and the Advertising Media

On August 28, 1922, when radio station WEAF in New York City charged $100.00 to allow employees of The Queensborough Corporation to read statements about the virtues of renting an apartment in a Jackson Heights development, radio became an advertising medium. These announcements are regarded as the first paid radio commercials in history. Prior to that time, some broadcast pioneers, such as RCA's David Sarnoff, believed that the radio industry would be supported by revenue from the sale of receivers. Others felt that the necessary income would be produced through fees paid by listeners either in the form of subscriptions, similar to those now paid for cable television service, or from taxes levied on the purchase or use of receivers, a practice common in Europe today.

But none of these possibilities were realized. The sale of time for advertising is now the chief source of revenue for commercial radio stations in the United States. Each station charges fees to broadcast commercials as part of its programming. The audience receives the programming and is exposed to the commercials. Through this process, advertisers seek to sell more of their products and services, the audience receives the programming without being directly charged, and the station tries to realize enough income to pay its expenses and give the owners a return on their investments. Although not without its detractors, this arrangement has served the public, business, and the radio industry well for years. With gross annual sales pushing $4 billion, radio is a major advertising medium.

Radio is many things to many people, but it must be a successful advertising medium to survive. Each radio station not only competes with the other stations in its market but with all of the other media operating in its market. Most advertisers have limited budgets with which to promote sales of their products and services through advertising. As a result, each selects those media that reach targeted audiences that match their targeted markets most effectively and efficiently. Since an advertiser considers each medium and various combinations of media to achieve its marketing goals, radio salespersons must be well prepared by knowing all aspects of their product and that of the competing media.

Though all of the advertising media have their strong points, radio has some decided advantages over the others. First and foremost, it offers one-on-one selling through the power and persuasiveness of words delivered by a human voice. No other medium is as immediate, timely, and flexible as radio. Each word of copy is used on the air. There is no small print, and nothing is glossed over. A commercial being broadcast by a station is the only programming being carried at that particular instant each time it is aired. It does not compete with 10 other ads on the same page. Radio reaches the members of the various targeted audiences both at home and away, no matter what else they may be doing at any time. Radio is efficient, provides broad reach, and has great impact on its audiences.

The total radio audience has become fragmented because of the existence of a large number of stations, the sophistication of listeners, and the increase in the variety of formats. In the past, each market contained at least one "must buy" radio station — the one all advertisers *had* to use in order to reach most of the audience most of the time. Very few, if any, "must buy" stations exist today. Aside from those in some very small, remote markets, no one station reaches the entire audience in its market. Each station's format is designed to capture and retain a particular segment of the audience. With the exceptin of events of national importance like the World Series, the Super Bowl, and space shots, no single program or series of programs captures a significant portion of the total national radio audience at any particular time.

The fragmentation of the radio audience has had a great impact on radio sales. The choices confronting advertisers are complex and difficult. As a result, the staff of the sales department of each station, to be effective, must (1) possess knowledge of the strengths and dimensions of both radio generally and its station specifically; (2) understand all competing media in its market; (3) have considerable expertise in retailing, advertising, and business generally, and (4) be capable of analyzing and solving marketing problems for each client through research, media planning, preparation of copy, and production abilities.

The Sales Department

Most people interested in a career in radio are initially attracted to programming. The prospect of being on the air acts as a powerful magnet that draws hopefuls into the business. While some aspirants begin their careers in radio in a sales department, many think of working there only after they learn (or are told) they are not cut out for programming. This situation is, however, changing. A career in sales is now recognized as the quickest route to a position in management. Most general managers today are alumni of sales departments. In addition, sales personnel are the best paid in the radio industry, with the exception of some top major market on-air performers.

Radio sales consist of three separate categories: local, national-regional (also called "spot sales"), and network. About 75 percent of the income of the average station is derived from local advertising, business from advertisers and agencies located within a 50 mile radius of the station; approximately 20 percent is national and regional business produced by the station's national sales representative (discussed hereafter), and regional and national networks provide five percent. These proportions vary from station to station.

The character and size of a station's sales department depend on many factors, such as the nature of its market, its ratings, and the prerogatives of its owners and top management. A sales department is ordinarily headed by a chief executive called the *general sales manager, sales director,* or *commercial manager.* Most stations appoint a *national sales director* to coordinate all sales efforts other than local in nature. The sales department staff consists of *salespersons* or *account executives* and *copywriters.* As might be expected, there are no hard and fast rules concerning the staffing of sales departments. For example, a general manager may also serve as general sales manager or a station may employ a full-time general sales manager. Still other stations may designate a salesperson to do the basic administrative tasks of a general sales manager as an extra responsibility.

The General Sales Manager

The principal job of the general sales manager is to generate as much income as possible for a commercial radio station. He reports directly to the general manager whose main responsibility, aside from preserving the broadcast license, is finding ways for the station to keep as much of that income as possible.

As the architect of the sales department, the general sales manager must create an organization which produces the maximum revenue for the station's product. While that product — programming — is the station's direct contact with the targeted audience, its sales force is its direct contact with local agencies and businesses, especially those which depend on advertising to sell their goods and services. The general sales manager seeks to mold the station's product and targeted audience into a saleable package that gets good results for its advertisers.

The general sales manager is responsible for every aspect of the station's sales efforts. He must be a good supervisor who oversees all sales personnel. He has to be creative and innovative in developing sales promotions through cooperation with the program director, production director, and the rest of the station's staff. It is essential that he maintain constant contacts with national, regional, and local agencies.

The position of general sales manager requires an intelligent, resourceful person, capable of obtaining market and media information from many sources. He must be skilled in using ratings and demonstrating the successful results achieved for advertisers by his station. He is also a human computer whose memory bank contains vital data regarding the market's area, demographics, business community, political activities, and trends. He should understand every aspect of the station's operation and capabilities, not just those of the sales department. From his vast sales experience, he should have mastered all legitimate techniques used to sell time, to service the station's clients properly, and to convey his knowledge and sales philosophy to each member of the sales staff.

A general sales manager has to be familiar with the techniques used by other media which compete with radio. This experience allows him to make comparisons between radio and the other media in ways that benefits his station. He also needs a solid retailing and marketing background to get the best possible results for clients through the use of radio.

Good people are needed to create and maintain an effective sales organization. The general sales manager must develop a system under which the best available prospects are recruited and hired. Every member of the staff must be imbued with the proper attitudes, understand the goals of the radio station, and be thoroughly familiar with what he is expected to accomplish by the general sales manager. In addition, each has to understand the legal restraints placed on sales, especially those dealing with lotteries, false and misleading ads, and double billing, an illegal practice by which excessive rates are charged. Before going into the marketplace, a new staff member should be properly trained and equipped to achieve success in sales. Once in the field, each staff member should be monitored, coached, and motivated to obtain good results for himself and the station.

The Salesperson

To succeed in radio, a salesperson or account executive must *want* to sell. Experience in and knowledge of selling are important, but it is very difficult to win at this game without the will to win. He has to love to sell because his task is formidable. He has the job of selling an intangible — something that has no tires to kick or parts to demonstrate. He must pitch a concept and convey his own genuine enthusiasm for radio to the client.

A salesperson is a money ballplayer. His successful efforts are converted directly into income. As a novice, he usually works on a salary basis until he learns his trade. Thereafter, he earns commissions on his sales which are paid by draws against those commissions.

A salesperson should have enthusiasm for his work, must project a pleasing and confident personality, and ought to be outgoing, but not obnoxious. He has to relish meeting people and should have the ability to get along with them. He should, however, avoid conduct and cliched speech which produces the stereotyped image from which "salesmen" suffer. Personal integrity is vital to success. Without the respect of the client, he is unable to develop a meaningful relationship with it. He must have a general appearance that reflects his personal warmth, sincerity, and credibility. He also must know the economic, social, and political facts of life about his market.

People in radio sales deal both with agencies and directly with clients. The agency personnel are familiar with all aspects of the marketing and media world, including the code words used in the business. Working with the client — direct selling — demands a close and continuing relationship. The client is usually not an advertising expert. His true interest is his own business. He usually can't waste time with advertising language, but uses advertising to solve problems, expand his business, and increase profits. The client involved in direct selling relies on the salesperson as a marketing and media consultant and has to be shown how radio generally and the station specifically will work for him.

To achieve his goal — full spectrum service to the client — the salesperson must, first and foremost, know radio and believe in it. He must have the facts and figures about his own station, competing stations, and other media in the market. He needs to have a thorough knowledge of audience research, surveys, and ratings in order to get his message across to the client. He also should be prepared to respond intelligently to the claims made by the competition with facts, not merely snipes. Comparisons with other stations' performances and targeted audiences as they relate to the client's business are his most potent weapons provided the facts used are accurate and legitimate.

Simply making the sale is not the end of the job for a salesperson. Anyone in the business might get lucky and hit a big one. But to retain a client, he must work hard and study every aspect of its business and industry. By means of a comprehensive analysis of the client's products or services and its targeted market, the salesperson identifies its needs and presents an advertising program designed to satisfy them.

Great sales in radio do not happen by accident. They are earned. The meticulous analysis of every aspect of the situation — doing all of the homework — pays off. Once the sale is closed, the effective salesperson stays with the deal by guiding implementation of the advertising plan, following up on the results, and suggesting adjustments to improve results in the future. This follow-up paves the way for a relationship that lasts a great deal longer than one sale.

In some situations, the sale of radio advertising is not in the best interests of a client, the salesperson, or the station. For example, if a client has a limited budget which prevents its purchasing a sufficient number of commercials to sell its product or service effectively, it won't get good results. A sale of time under these circumstances is shortsighted and bad for all parties. The client will get poor results for which it will inevitably blame the salesperson and the station. An unhappy client seldom suffers silently. This type of situation should be avoided by not selling any time to the client.

The salesperson should be able to write decent copy and recommend production methods. Some experience selling intangibles is helpful to a newcomer in radio sales, but not mandatory. A bright individual with drive who really wants to sell will make it big in radio sales.

The Copywriter

Radio commercials for national and regional advertisers are delivered to a radio station in neat packages provided by advertising agencies or departments. The copy for local advertising is prepared either by an agency or a *copywriter* employed by the station.

Unlike most other forms of advertising, the radio commercial is not built around an actual picture, scene, or headline put together by an art director "in living color." But radio is probably the most visual of all media. Using words, sound, and music, the radio writer can create characters, situations, and even entire universes that could not be duplicated in print ads or television commercials. Through his imagination, the listener is able to project himself into any make-believe situation. A successful radio commercial depends upon the listener's participation. Since listeners are usually on the go and are being bombarded by salvos of commercials and advertisements day and night, the copywriter has a formidable task in trying to get them involved in a commercial. But it is done all the time.

A radio commercial starts with an idea, a plan, a distinctive sound, a jingle — anything necessary to hook the listener's attention. The appeal of the commercial may be direct or indirect, emotional or logical. Whatever the appeal, it is not selected by chance. It must meet the advertising objectives of the client and is determined through knowing the client, its product or service, and the targeted audience.

Some radio commercials are still done live, but most are recorded. They consist of words, sound, and music, and are produced in many formats, too numerous to catalogue fully here. Some of the most prominent formats use story lines, testimonials, analogies, fantasies, jingles, and personalities. But no matter what the format, an effective commercial must carry a message of importance to which the listener relates. The salesperson sells the client, but the copywriter must build a commercial that convinces the targeted audience with a message that: (1) delivers the advertiser's message effectively; (2) is done in good taste, and (3) stays within the legal limits established by the law dealing with false and misleading advertising.

Whether he works at it on a full-time basis or has other functions within the radio station, the copywriter must have an excellent command of the language, considerable advertising expertise, and a solid radio background. In addition, he should be aware of the state of the art concerning radio technology. The tools used in production of commercials are highly sophisticated and provide great creative latitude through electronic mixing and editing. A background in psychology is also very useful.

National Sales Representatives

Each radio station needs income from sales to businesses and agencies located outside its market. Where used here, the term "national business" means all sales of advertising that are not local. With the exception of some major market stations which maintain sales offices in New York, Chicago, and Los Angeles, and those which are members of group operations, radio stations depend on national sales representatives to negotiate, service, and follow up on this type of business.

Prior to the early 1930's, no organized method of station representation existed. While certain advertising agencies and radio time brokers attempted to fill the gap, the absence of responsible, ethical firms dealing specifically with the placement of national business resulted in a chaotic situation. In 1932, Edward Petry organized the first modern firm that legitimately represented stations across the country and brought some sense to this area. Today, more than 200 firms serve as *national reps* for radio stations.

A rep firm is not actually a member of a station's sales staff. It is, rather, a separate company that works as an additional sales force across the nation or region for each of its station clients. Major reps handle a large number of stations. At one time, it was considered inappropriate for a rep to handle more than one station in each market. Today, a firm may handle two or more stations in the same market as long as they do not use the same format.

Being represented by a major rep is critical to a radio station. Its ability to get national business is impaired unless it has a top rep. As a result, the demand for such firms is great. Some reps insist upon and get compensation that is a fixed percentage of *all* station sales, whether national, regional, or local, even though the reps did not produce all of those sales. Other rep firms work for commissions based on national business they obtain. They are generally paid a sum equal to 15 percent of the net revenue received by the station for the time they sell. Since an agency generally takes a commission of 15 percent of the gross amount billed by a station for the advertising time it orders, the rep receives 15 percent of 85 percent, or 12.75 percent of the billings. Some group stations represent themselves and, at the same time, serve as reps for other noncompeting stations.

While all sales activities of a station are under the jurisdiction of the general sales manager, in larger stations a national sales director is appointed to work directly with the rep. He coordinates matters between the rep and the station and very often gets involved in actual sales presentations to prospective clients.

Like any good radio salesperson, a rep does his homework. He must be completely familiar with the station, its strengths, market, and targeted audience. The rep's efforts are coordinated with the station, and, accordingly, he must be equipped to sell the station, service the advertiser, and follow up on each account. The sales staff member responsible for national and regional sales must constantly provide the rep with all the information and material needed to complete sales and retain clients. Since a rep has the responsibility of selling the station, he must know its competition and is usually in a position to make recommendations which strengthen its market position.

Network Sales

As will be discussed in Chapter Ten, the status of network radio is changing dramatically. Many specialized and general programming networks have been established since 1979, and more are on the way. Linked by wire or satellite communication systems, the networks provide advertisers with a way to reach substantial numbers of listeners by radio at a comparatively low cost.

The business arrangements between radio networks and stations vary considerably. The relationship under which a network actually shares its revenue of time sales with its affiliated stations is a throwback to The Golden Age of Radio. The affiliate receives a payment per network commercial which is less than the rate per commercial usually charged local advertisers by the station. Under the more common arrangement used today, the programming provided the affiliate by the network contains commercials which have been sold by the network. The network retains all of the revenue generated by these commercials. The programming also contains slots or *availabilities* for sale by the local station to its own clients. It receives the programming for no direct charge and retains the income from the time it sells. Stations in larger markets also receive direct compensation from the networks to remain affiliated. Still other networks act as syndicators and are paid to provide programming to local stations.

It is clear that radio networks are destined to become again a dynamic force in the industry. Only the future will demonstrate the shape and direction of that force.

Chapter Nine

Radio Engineering

Radio began as a collection of scientific theories, experiments, and discoveries. But engineers took it from the laboratory and produced a phenomenon which quickly captured the imaginations of millions. Through the practical broadcasting devices they created, radio not only revolutionized humankind's ability to communicate, but cleared the way for the development of other advances such as global communications, television, and space exploration. To those who understand and appreciate its theoretical and technical aspects, radio is a continuing source of amazement. To the rest of the world, it is a part of everyday life that is taken for granted.

Through their pioneering spirit and determination, engineers initiated regular radio service when they built numerous experimental stations around the United States in the early 1900's. They became the first announcers when they took to the airwaves to find out if their marvelous devices actually worked. Radio's commercial aspects became possible only after engineers developed it as a dependable and practical medium of communication. Thereafter, programming, sales, and management talent joined forces with the engineers to make commercial radio a dynamic force in our society.

The financial community awakened to the commercial possibilities of AM radio prior to 1920. At the time, the number of radio frequencies available for use in the United States was strictly limited by international agreements which allocated portions of the total radio spectrum for use by the Americas. Although the agreements controlled the number of frequencies that were available, the way those frequencies were used within the United States was not regulated. Federal law merely required that each new station file a notice with the Bureau of Standards of the Department of Commerce before going on the air. New stations were created daily. As soon as one went on the air, it quickly attracted an audience. The airwaves were so crowded that stations actually shared frequencies. Some used as many as three frequencies during each day. As the number of stations increased, it was common for two or more with closely situated transmitters to

Transmitting tower and antenna of W2XMN, the first full-scale, 50kW FM radio station, built by the developer of FM, Edwin H. Armstrong, near Alpine, New Jersey in 1939. The age of high fidelity in radio and sound reproduction began with this station. *Courtesy of Armstrong Foundation.*

broadcast simultaneously on the same or adjacent frequencies with little regard for the interference their signals produced. Some station owners did anything possible to boost their signals to dominate the electromagnetic jungle they created.

Responsible broadcasters and government officials realized that unless some order was brought to the uncontrolled use of frequencies, the infant radio industry would soon destroy itself. In 1927, Congress created the Federal Radio Commission which moved quickly to stabilize and regulate the use of frequencies. It set up the forerunner of today's system of AM radio station classification to reduce interference and provide the most widespread service to the general public. Specific frequency assignments, hours of operation, and power limits were established and strictly enforced. Far fewer stations were allowed to broadcast at night when radio waves travel farther than during daytime and can cause interference.

Two principles have been the basis of radio regulation in this country: First, radio broadcasting facilities must be used to serve best the "public interest, convenience, and necessity;" Second, the radio spectrum is a natural resource which is the property of the general public. As a result, no one may *own* a radio frequency. Rather, each station licensee is granted a qualified right to use a specific frequency under various terms. As long as the station licensee serves the public and operates within the rules and regulations of the FCC and the terms of its license, that right will be renewed. Failure to comply with these requirements could result in the loss of the broadcast license or other heavy penalties.

Radio Station Operator Licenses

With the advent of regulation, the role of the radio engineer changed dramatically. Each station licensee became ultimately responsible for all aspects of the operation of the station. Specific, objective, and tough technical standards set by the FCC had to be maintained by every station. Then, as now, most station licensees were businessmen, not engineers. They neither had the training nor experience alone to keep their stations in compliance with the new technical requirements established under the Communications Act of 1934 ("Act"). The engineer, once a jack-of-all-trades, became the radio station operator and technical specialist whose knowledge and abilities were vital to the existence of each station.

The Act gave the FCC the authority to set the qualifications of station operators, to classify them in accordance with the duties they perform, and to issue commercial operator licenses and permits to United States citizens and nationals.

The following analogy illustrates the relationship between a station licensee and its licensed operators. A station license is in many respects like a motor vehicle registration. Almost anyone may own such a vehicle, but it may by used on the public roads only after a registration is issued by the state. It assigns a unique combination of letters and numbers to the vehicle (license plate), states the uses allowed for the vehicle (passenger, commercial, livery, etc.), and imposes the requirement that the registrant use the vehicle in compliance with all of the rules and regulations of the motor vehicle code. Similarly, a station license assigns a unique station identification in the form of call letters, states the authorized uses of the station (broadcasting, marine, aviation, etc.), and requires that the station licensee comply with all FCC rules and the terms of the license.

To continue with the analogy, it is not enough for the owner to have a motor vehicle registration. If the vehicle is to be driven on public roads, it must be under the control of someone who has a personal operator's license. Other passengers in the vehicle may use or adjust certain equipment, such as the radio, heater, or windshield wipers, but the essential functions — accelerating, steering, and braking — must be under the direct control of the licensed operator. Whenever a radio station is "on the air," it must be under the control of a licensed operator. Other, unlicensed persons may use the microphones (announce), run turntables, edit newscasts, etc., but the hour-by-hour technical control of the transmitting system involving audio volume levels, output power, and, in some cases, antenna pattern are the responsibilities of the licensed operator.

Under the Act, the FCC established a testing and classification procedure by which qualified engineers were granted various operator licenses and permits on the basis of their professional abilities. Certain engineering tasks and requirements specified in the FCC rules and regulations could only be performed by operators holding the highest class of license. Although this procedure was no guaranty to a station licensee that a particular engineer was a competent operator, it was an indication that the holder of a particular operator license or permit had studied and understood the regulations to the satisfaction of the FCC.

Until recently, the FCC issued four types of operator licenses and permits relating to AM and FM broadcast stations. They were:

1. First Class Radiotelephone Operator License.

2. Second Class Radiotelephone Operator License.

3. Third Class Radiotelephone Operator Permit.

4. Restricted Radiotelephone Operator Permit.

The first class operator license was the highest issued by the FCC. All stations had to employ at least one full-time engineer holding a

"first class ticket" or, under certain circumstances, contract in writing
for the services of one or more such engineers on a part-time basis.
Only first class operators were authorized to perform transmitter
maintenance and repair. Each station had to have a first class operator
available in the event of a transmitter problem. A second or third class
ticket holder could not make any transmitter internal adjustments
except under the direct supervision of a first class engineer. A first class
operator was also required to perform a number of inspections of the
facilities of the station throughout the year. He was responsible for all
repairs and adjustments necessary to keep the station's operations in
compliance with the limits set forth in specific FCC rules and its license.

Applicants for first, second, and third class tickets were required to
take written examinations and receive a passing grade of 75 percent or
more. An applicant for a restricted permit was not required to take an
examination, but had to certify as to certain facts in his application.
The holders of such restricted permits (which included most on-air
performers) were strictly limited as to the technical tasks they could
perform at a radio station. They could, through external controls on
the equipment only, make adjustments which:

1. turned transmitters on and off;

2. compensated for voltage changes in the power supply;

3. maintained modulation of the transmitter within certain limits;

4. made routine changes in operating power which were required
   in the license, and

5. switched antenna positions to conform with required radiating
   patterns.

But the FCC's system for licensing radiotelephone operators became
obsolete because it failed to keep pace with technical developments.
Recognizing that modern broadcast transmitting equipment is much
more stable and reliable than its predecessors, the FCC deregulated
operator requirements. It eliminated the Radiotelephone Third Class
Operator Permit in 1980. Persons holding third class tickets were
advised to obtain either a Restricted Radiotelephone Operator Permit
for use in AM and FM radio broadcasting or a Marine Radio Operator
for use in the maritime area only.

The greatest changes in the licensing of operators became effective
August 7, 1981, when the FCC authorized operators holding *any* class
of commercial radio license or permit (including the Restricted Radiotelephone Operator Permit, but excluding the Marine Radio Operator
Permit) to perform all technical duties at commercial radio stations.
This includes the installation, maintenance, repair, and technical supervision of AM and FM transmitting equipment. The First Class Radio-

Modern, compact AM transmitter. *Courtesy of Harris Corporation.*

telephone Operator License was eliminated, and the Second Class Radiotelephone Operator License became the General Radiotelephone Operator License. As a result, the FCC now issues only two classes of radiotelephone licenses or permits — the General Radiotelephone Operator License and the Restricted Radiotelephone Operator Permit.

To obtain the General Radiotelephone Operator License, an applicant must be a person legally employable in the United States; be able to receive and transmit spoken messages in English, and pass an FCC written examination consisting of three sections known as Element 1 (Basic Law), Element 2 (Basic Operator Procedure), and Element 3 (Basic Radiotelephone). Element 3 is a 100 question multiple-choice examination which covers many topics. An applicant must receive a grade of 75 percent or more to pass the examination.

The Restricted Radiotelephone Operator Permit is granted without an examination. To be eligible for the permit, a person legally employable in the United States must be at least 14 years of age and certify that he:

1. has a need for the permit;

2. can keep at least a rough written log;

3. is familiar with the provisions of applicable treaties, laws, and rules and regulations governing the radio station which he will be the operator;

4. will keep current with the treaties, laws, and rules and regulations, and

5. will preserve the secrecy of radio communications not intended for use by the general public.

In announcing the relaxation of operator requirements, the FCC emphasized that each station licensee continues to be responsible for all aspects of the station. While it intended to reduce the volume and burden of regulation imposed on station licensees, the FCC did not ease their responsibilities to insure that their stations operate in strict compliance with the rules.

Each station now must have at least one person holding a general or restricted ticket in charge of the transmitter during all periods of broadcast operation. That operator must be positioned either at the transmitter location, a remote control point, an automatic transmission system monitor and alarm point, or a place where extension meters are installed for monitoring the condition of the transmitter. He must be able to observe the required transmitter and monitor metering to determine any deviations from the norm and also be able to make the necessary adjustments from his normal duty position. The operator on duty at a transmitter may perform other tasks at the radio station provided they do not interfere with his proper operation of the broadcast transmission system.

Each station licensee must designate a person holding a general or restricted ticket to serve as the station's *chief operator*. The licensee must also designate another to serve as the *acting chief operator* when the chief operator is not available or able to act. The chief operator of an AM station using a directional antenna or operating with greater than 10 kW authorized power must be an employee of the station and available for duty for whatever number of hours each week the station licensee determines is necessary to keep the station's technical operation in compliance with the FCC rules and the terms of the station's license. The chief operator of a non-directional AM station operating with authorized power not exceeding 10 kW or for any FM station may either be an employee of the station or an individual or firm engaged to serve on a contract basis for whatever number of hours each week the licensee determines is necessary to keep the station's technical operation in compliance.

The designation of a person as a station's chief operator or the appointment of a chief operator serving on a contract basis both must be in writing and on file in the station. Such a designation need not be filed with the FCC, but must be readily available to an FCC inspector. The chief operator has the specific responsibility to:

1. conduct weekly (or monthly in the case of stations using automatic transmitting systems) inspections and calibrations of the transmission system, required monitors, metering and control systems, and make any necessary repairs or adjustments as needed;

2. make or supervise periodic AM field monitoring point measurements, equipment performance measurements, or other tests as specified in the FCC rules and regulations and the terms of the station's license;

3. review the station operating logs at least once a week as part of the transmission system inspections to determine if the entries are being made correctly or if the station has been operating as required by the FCC rules and regulations and the terms of the station's license; upon completion of the review, he must make a notation of the discrepancies observed, date and sign the log, and initiate necessary corrective action as may be required, and

4. make or supervise entries in the maintenance log.

The Engineering Department

Few broadcasters who work in programming, sales, and management are qualified engineers. Most do not understand the differences between a stereo generator and a frequency monitor, but they all know when to call the engineering department — usually when something doesn't work. The efforts of engineers are seldom appreciated until the push of a button fails to start a cartridge machine or the demon "dead air" rears its ugly head. Fortunately, the industry has many highly qualified and dedicated technicians who keep things working most of the time.

A station's technical complexity is dictated by a number of factors including its type, class, market, and competition. To meet its competition, a station tries to provide its audience with the best sound and service possible within its financial abilities. There is virtually no limit to the technical equipment each station *could* use to enhance its sound and service — elaborate remote facilities, modern mobile units, satellite downlinks, etc. But a station is a business, and expenditures for equipment and everything else must be in proportion to its revenue.

State-of-the-art stereophonic modular audio console. *Courtesy of Harris Corporation.*

The size and makeup of a station's engineering department are reflections of its technical complexity. Small stations often do not have their own technical staffs. They rely on part-time contract engineers to do all of their maintenance and repair work. These technical specialists possess the appropriate licenses and usually service a number of commercial and non-commercial stations within the same market. In some small and medium size stations, management and other staff members perform routine technical tasks, but specialists are brought in to maintain and repair the transmitting systems. Large stations need sophisticated engineering organizations to keep them on the air, to meet all FCC operational requirements, and to satisfy the demands of all of their departments. Under deregulation, the FCC has practically given each station's management a free hand to staff its engineering department in any way it chooses, provided its own strict technical standards are met.

Since technical complexities and staff makeups vary greatly from station to station, it is impossible to define an "average" engineering department. But every engineering staff, whatever its composition, deals daily with a myriad of technical matters, some mandated by the FCC and others which consist of routine maintenance and repair work of all types and descriptions. A great deal of its efforts are expended to monitor and sustain the following essential broadcast equipment:

Transmitting System — the heart of the technical operation of a radio station. It consists of transmitters, frequency and modulation monitors, limiting amplifiers, stereo generators, and other devices.

Antenna System — basically a tower or array of towers, a ground system (AM only), phasing components, and lighting facilities required under both FCC and Federal Aviation Authority regulations.

Studio Equipment — audio consoles, microphones, speakers, sound reproducing devices, such as turntables, tape decks and cartridge machines, and other facilities used to broadcast and record.

Two-way Radio System — a separately licensed radio channel, a base station, and mobile units that are used for on-the-spot reporting and remote broadcasts.

Test Equipment — field strength meters, tube testers, and devices which measure audio output, radio frequencies, and the quality of the performance of various items of equipment.

Microwave Links — a separately licensed point-to-point radio system that replaces telephone lines in the sending of program material from the studio to the transmitter.

As part of its technical responsibilities, the engineering department is required by the FCC to keep extensive records and complete the following paper work:

Transmitter Operating Log — various transmitter meter readings taken by a licensed operator at intervals not exceeding three hours. Automated meter readings are also permitted.

Weekly Inspection and Maintenance Log — a record of required examinations and service of transmitting equipment which must be performed by a holder of a General Radiotelephone Operator License.

Quarterly Tower Light Inspection Report — a statement of the condition of the tower lights and related control devices that automatically turn the lights on and off at sundown and sunup.

Monthly Frequency Check — a record of the readings of a monitor which measures the signal being transmitted by a station. It is used to determine if the actual frequency is too high or too low. AM frequencies are permitted to deviate by 20 Hz up or down. For example, if a station were assigned the frequency of 1300 kHz, frequency fluctuations between 1,300,020 Hz and 1,299,980 Hz would be permissible. In FM, fluctuations of 2,000 Hz up or down are allowed.

Annual Proof of Performance Report — a check of a station's frequency response, noise, and distortion. A "frequency response" is a measurement of the abilities of a station's audio and transmitting devices to reproduce sound faithfully. "Noise" is the amount of unwanted sound such as cross talk, static, etc., generated and put on the transmitter carrier by studio equipment, the transmitter itself, or by the studio-to-transmitter link. The term "distortion" is a measurement of any unwanted side effects generated by broadcast equipment which were not present in the original audio. The FCC rules set forth the details of the measurements and performance requirements.

In addition to the work of maintaining all broadcast equipment and keeping a station in compliance with FCC requirements, an engineering department is also responsible for other equipment and facilities of the station not directly involved in broadcast operations. As a result, a technical staff must consist of individuals who possess widely varied abilities and experience in many areas. Where a station has its own engineering department, it is usually headed by an executive called the *chief engineer*. Other titles used to describe this position are *director of engineering services* and *director of technical operations*. His staff consists of *engineers* and *technicians*.

The Chief Engineer

The principal goal of a chief engineer is achieving and sustaining his station's technical excellence. He must keep the station on the air and establish systems which insure its compliance with all FCC rules, its license, and the standards of good engineering practices. To succeed at his job, he must be both a technical wizard and an outstanding administrator.

Keeping a station on the air requires continual inspection, maintenance, and replacement of key broadcast equipment plus the development of backup facilities for use in the event of breakdowns. The chief engineer must get the maximum life out of existing equipment and replace worn or obsolete gear before it causes any interruption in broadcast service. Many dynamic developments have occurred in the field of broadcast equipment through the use of transistors, computers, digital and other types of technology. Modern equipment, being more dependable and requiring less maintenance, has significantly improved the operational efficiency of most stations. A chief engineer has to stay current with all of these developments by reviewing literature, attending conventions, and working with competent equipment specialists.

As the station's "chief operator," the chief engineer is responsible for the station's compliance with all FCC requirements. He schedules the inspections and maintenance of transmitting equipment, oversees the keeping of all logs and records, and supervises the "running" of the station by qualified licensed operators. He also has the obligation of being informed about all regulatory developments which have an impact on his station. Some of the technical situations he faces are beyond his own training and experience. He will often call in an engineering consultant for advice on equipment and regulatory matters.

The responsibilities of a chief engineer go far beyond keeping a station on the air and complying with the rules. He is usually in charge of the entire physical plant of a station. His domain extends from practically every mechanical and electrical device used in each of the station's departments to all of the buildings and grounds involved in the operations of the station, including studio and transmitting buildings, antennas, parking areas, and the security measures each requires.

As is the case in every other aspect of radio, the efforts of a number of people are needed to accomplish the work of an engineering department. A chief engineer can not do it alone. To fulfill his diverse and numerous responsibilities, he must be a leader who inspires those about him to meet his high engineering standards. A chief engineer usually creates good relationships with local technical schools and engineering colleges so that the station is assured of a supply of recruits in the event an opening develops on his staff.

A chief engineer has to be a good communicator to be effective in his job. He must, as part of the training of his staff, provide a clear statement of his standards and procedures and insist upon disciplined maintenance. For dealing with department heads and their staffs, he should develop the knack of translating the highly technical language of his department into terms understandable by nonengineers. He is headed for trouble if he can't "keep it simple." For example, many stations use combination announcer-operators. As holders of restricted tickets, they are usually not well versed in electronic theory. But the station and its general manager depend upon them to perform vital functions. As a result, all explanations given to announcer-operators should be done in nontechnical words.

Every general manager is concerned about the way his station meets FCC technical standards. A chief engineer must keep his general manager informed of anything pertaining to technical changes in FCC regulations, new developments in broadcast equipment, and any regulatory or staff problem of the station.

It is apparent that a competent chief engineer must be more than a specialist in broadcast equipment. He has to be a professional with a finely honed knowledge of all aspects of radio. His standards of engineering excellence must be high. He has to be dedicated to his station and perfecting its sound. He must, however, have both an awareness of the economics of radio and an interest in the accomplishment of all the goals of the station. But he must not lower those standards. He is usually the only one capable of keeping a station technically honest. If he fails, the station will wind up in deep trouble because, unlike broadcast equipment, there is no backup for him.

The Chief Engineer's Staff

While the size and makeup of the staff of every engineering department varies due to many factors, each performs transmitter, maintenance, and audio services. In small stations, all of the services are performed by each staff member, and in larger operations, the engineering staff consists of specialists in each of these areas.

A transmitter engineer is a specialist who has the training and experience to handle all aspects of a transmitting system. A maintenance engineer is the closest thing to a jack-of-all-trades on the staff. He divides his time between broadcast and other equipment and facilities at the station. Like a transmitter engineer, his orientation is technical.

The audio engineer controls a console or board during broadcast and recording sessions. He operates in a pressurized environment and must remain cool at all times. He has to be alert and quick-witted, have the ability to react instantly, and routinely handle emergencies. He also must be able to take instructions, operate his board and related equipment, and think ahead for the next development simultaneously. He works with on-air performers of varying temperaments and styles. To serve them well, he must study their approaches and learn how to anticipate their moves. It is apparent that his abilities are more operational than technical. Many on-air performers today serve as their own audio engineers.

Earth station satellite antenna measuring 6.1 meters. *Courtesy of Harris Corporation.*

Chapter Ten

Network Radio

America's first commercial radio stations developed from amateur experimental transmitters. Each produced its own programming and served a local area. When order was finally brought to the airwaves through Federal regulation in the 1920's, some stations were authorized to transmit with higher power and, as a result, provided regional coverage. The development of a broadcast system capable of reaching the entire country was the next logical step in the extension of radio service. Thus, national network radio was born.

Prior to 1920, informal networks were set up for short periods of time when stations occasionally provided programming to each other. Thereafter, special temporary networks — some involving two or three stations, and others interconnecting coast-to-coast chains of dozens of stations — were strung together for special news, sports, or entertainment broadcasts. American Telephone and Telegraph Company (AT&T) set up the first network that provided regularly scheduled programming. Using radio station WEAF in New York City as its base of operations, AT&T provided entertainment programming that featured the biggest names in show business several hours a week across the nation over its web of telephone lines.

The Golden Age of Radio arrived with the establishment of the National Broadcasting Company (NBC). On November 15, 1926, it signed on the air with an elaborate four hour show before a live, formally attired studio audience of 1,000 people. Originating from the Waldorf Astoria Hotel in New York City, the program featured speeches by dignitaries and performances by stars of the Metropolitan Opera, five orchestras, a brass band, and many other acts. Humorist Will Rogers also appeared via a remote broadcast from Missouri. More than 2.5 million people heard this first broadcast over what NBC called the Red Network. Two months later, NBC launched the Blue Network, a second national service which produced its own programming and had a separate lineup of affiliates.

NBC's two networks soon faced tough competition. The Columbia Broadcasting System (CBS) inaugurated its own network in 1927. The

Mutual Broadcasting System (MBS) began operating in 1934. The FCC, in a move designed to prevent a monopoly of network service, adopted rules in 1941 which prohibited any firm from owning more than one network. Being forced to dispose of one of its networks under these rules, NBC sold the Blue Network in 1943 to a group of businessmen who developed it as the American Broadcasting Company (ABC). The FCC reversed the rules against multiple network ownership in 1968 and, as a result, ushered in a second era of prominence for network radio. At that time, ABC was granted permission to operate four separate networks, each serving a specific targeted audience through specialized formats.

With its earlier technical problems solved, radio began to attract large audiences on a regular basis to its network programs. As the networks developed, the industry emerged as a successful medium of mass advertising. New national programming formats featuring big name personalities and acts were shaped into vehicles attractive to advertisers who responded by supporting the networks. Since the costs of these major entertainment shows were well beyond the means of local stations, the four major networks dominated the industry through the 1950's. Practically every commercial station was dependent upon a network affiliation for its survival. In 1941, the networks accounted for over 50 percent of all radio advertising revenue, and 700 of the 850 commercial stations on the air were affiliated with one of the four major networks.

But a succession of events between 1948 and 1960 ended the domination of the industry by the networks. First, the FCC reduced the spacing requirements between AM frequencies, thus allowing numerous stations throughout the nation to share frequencies without interfering with one another. This action caused a dynamic increase in the number of AM stations. By 1952, more than 3,000 such stations were licensed and on the air. Second, the FCC started to authorize FM frequencies, and more than 600 such stations went on the air. Although not an instant success, FM flourished in the 1970's. Third, the FCC started the television boom in 1952 when it lifted a freeze on new stations and authorized additional VHF and UHF outlets to be constructed. The number of television stations on the air across the country went from 108 to 441 by 1956. In the wake of these developments, the Golden Age of Radio became a memory.

The entire radio industry in the United States suffered a deep recession in 1960, and the networks were the hardest hit. They generated a mere five percent of the total radio advertising revenue that year and provided very limited broadcast services. Aside from news and sports programming, they offered little else to the public and potential affiliates. Local radio quickly recovered from that point and has since enjoyed its greatest period of economic growth. Recent technological and business developments have paved the way for a comeback by network radio.

Satellites Boost Network Radio

Network radio, yesterday's most important medium, is showing positive signs of renewed growth and importance. Many believe the industry is at the dawn of a new era. And the development of dynamic technology has hastened its return to prominence. From their beginnings, the networks were dependent on landlines to relay programming from point to point and to interconnect their affiliates. Landlines are owned by the various telephone companies and leased to the networks at high rates. The use of landlines is expensive because many relays are required to transmit signals long distances in this fashion. Since they deteriorate when passed through multiple relays, signals require complicated electronic devices to retain levels of quality suitable for broadcast.

The emancipation of the networks from their reliance on landlines began when Congress enacted the Communications Satellite Act of 1962. Under this legislation, the FCC was given authority over satellite communication systems in space, directed to hasten their use in the relaying of telecommunication information, and ordered to insure effective competition for the establishment and operation of these systems. Congress also established COMSAT, a publicly owned corporation, with the mission of creating civilian communications satellite systems. COMSAT has achieved its goal. Satellites are now an economical method for the distribution of radio and television programs with high fidelity signal transmissions and broad multi-point nationwide coverage.

A network distributes its programming through a communications satellite system by delivering its signal through a local landline or loop to an uplink, an earth transmitting station consisting of a dish type antenna. The uplink beams the signal to the satellite which is in a geosynchronous orbit 22,300 miles above the equator. The satellite appears to remain in a fixed position in space because it revolves with the earth rather than around it. It makes one orbit during the time —one day — that the earth makes one rotation on its axis. If the satellite could be seen from the ground, it would seem to remain stationary, but it actually is orbiting at a tremendous speed.

The signal from an uplink is transmitted on a specific frequency to which a transponder (a combination receiver and transmitter) on board the satellite is tuned. The signal is automatically transmitted by the transponder back toward the earth on a different frequency in a pattern which covers approximately one-third of the planet's surface. That signal, called a footprint, may be received by any number of downlinks, earth receiving antennas, located throughout the United States. Each downlink contains a demodulator which separates the network's signal from the various other signals being transmitted from the satellite. From each downlink location, the signal is delivered via local loops or microwave links to radio stations affiliated with the network for broadcast to their respective audiences. A growing number of stations are installing their own downlinks, thereby reducing their costs and eliminating dependence on local loops or microwave connections. The diagram on the following page illustrates the various components of a communications satellite system.

Modern Network Radio

The new era of network radio began with the regulatory about-face by the FCC in 1968. ABC radio was granted permission to split into four separate networks — Contemporary, Entertainment, FM, and Information — each aimed at a specific demographic group. This action effectively set aside the rules prohibiting the ownership of multiple networks by a single firm and cleared the way for the establishment of many new networks.

Shortly after the ABC decision, NBC launched its News and Information Service in addition to its regular radio network. The ABC concept of four separate networks has flourished, while the NBC second network failed. Both efforts are significant because they marked the beginning of a trend to orient radio networks on demographic bases. That trend has been gaining momentum.

Network radio — the elder statesman of the electronic media — has, in many respects, emerged as a new industry, built not only on the multichannel capacity of satellites, but on the needs of radio stations to be more than music boxes for their targeted audiences. Most of today's new networks are created and programmed to serve the needs of particular targeted audiences through high quality programming.

In the early days of the networks, each employed the same basic format to showcase virtually identical programming. Both networks and advertisers were then concerned mostly about the numbers of listeners attracted by programs rather than the audiences' demographic characteristics. The new networks are scientifically programmed to reach specific demographic cells and complement formats in use in local stations. They provide highly specialized programs, such as news services finely tailored for stations employing Album Oriented Rock, Beautiful Music, Adult Contemporary, and other formats; general programming directed at specific ethnic groups, and All Talk Shows. Other networks specialize in lifestyle presentations, religious programming, special events, sports, features, and every other conceivable shade of programming. Amidst all of this demographic pro-

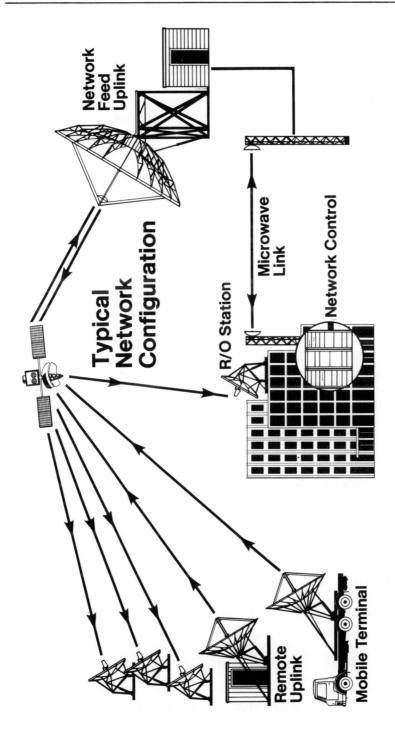

Typical radio network configuration showing applications within a satellite communications system. (Copyright © 1982. Scientific-Atlanta, Inc. All rights reserved. Reprinted by permission.)

gramming, some of the veteran networks, eschewing specialization, remain basically all things to all people by providing a wide selection of shows consisting of news, analyses, sports, features, dramatic presentations, and specials. And, in a throwback to yesteryear, special one-time networks for major sporting events are now put together with ease, thanks to satellite technology.

Demographic networking is not the exclusive territory of commercial radio. National Public Radio (NPR), a non-profit, private corporation, is a producer and distributor of programming intended to augment and enhance the broadcast schedules of local educational and public radio stations. NPR and its affiliates are dedicated to the creation of a broad spectrum of fine arts programming that is a unique service to the American public.

Network targeted audiences are selected in the same method pioneered by local stations. After an analysis of national population trends, considerable research, and a review of the programming and targeted audiences of the competition, a new network selects its targeted audience by locating a certain group of listeners presently not being served or one which is being poorly served by other networks. Once its audience is defined, the network seeks to develop programming that will attract and retain that audience.

Affiliates are the life's blood of a network. To be received by the general public, a network's programming must be carried on a number of strategically placed stations. The quality of its affiliates is particularly important. A network affiliated with a series of weak outlets across the nation is unable to reach a significant audience within each market. Unless it is affiliated with powerful stations in most of top 100 markets, a network's credibility as a national medium is suspect. In order to put together a prestigious lineup, some networks pay compensation directly to stations in certain major markets for being affiliates.

Networks and stations enter into written affiliation agreements which spell out the nature of the arrangements between them. Generally, a network agrees to provide its programming to an affiliate without charge. The affiliate, in return, agrees to carry or clear all or part of the network's programming, including the advertising it contains. Aside from the compensation discussed above, most affiliates are usually not paid for carrying a network's advertising, but are given availabilities within which they may insert the advertising they have sold to their own clients.

Network Administration and Management

A radio network engages in the same basic activities as does an individual station — the production and distribution of programming and the sale of time to advertisers. Its employees work in management, programming, sales, and engineering, and in other departments, unique to networks such as affiliate affairs and network owned and operated stations.

The top management of a network establishes the general policies which control the overall direction and guide the operation of the enterprise. While titles vary, each network is usually run by a president, its chief executive officer, and his subordinates, ordinarily vice presidents, who head divisions which deal with programming, sales, affiliate affairs, owned and operated stations, engineering, finance, planning and analysis, public relations and advertising, program standards, and legal affairs.

The very best network programming is of little value unless it is carried by a substantial number of top affiliates and is received by an audience which advertisers want to reach. The affiliate affairs division is responsible for the quality and quantity of the lineup of stations that broadcast a network's offerings. Its staff courts and signs affiliates to agreements, secures clearances for network programming, keeps the affiliates informed about network activities, makes all technical arrangements, and resolves scheduling and other conflicts that arise from time to time.

Unlike an individual radio station, a network is not subject to extensive regulation. The FCC does require that the operator of an uplink transmitter obtain a license, but most networks hire licensed firms for this particular service. No license is needed to use other satellite facilities such as the satellite itself or the downlink. Since a network provides programming that is carried by individual stations, great care must be taken to prevent the feeding of any programming by the network which, if carried by a station, would violate FCC regulations and place its license in jeopardy.

The programming of a network is created to attract and retain its targeted audience and affiliates. Its programming personnel plan and produce both regularly scheduled programs and coverage of national and international special events. Each network produces programs at its own cost, and, as a result, those affiliates which carry substantial network programming achieve considerable savings in their operating budgets. In addition, most of the network programming is of the type and quality no affiliate could afford to produce by itself. An affiliate does, however, forego the income it could have generated had it sold the availabilities surrendered to the network in exchange for the programming.

Most of the divisions of a network are more complex than their counterparts in local stations because it has a large, far-flung audience, produces more complex programming, and is dependent on its affiliates for the delivery of its product. In the case of sales, the network account executive must work with a national sales rep and many advertising agencies in order to plan and execute a national sales campaign for an advertiser. Although on a larger scale, network sales are made, as they are in local radio, when the account executive does his homework.

Operations and engineering personnel handle all of the technical needs of a network. They are responsible for the maintenance and operation of studios, facilities, and equipment used in remote broadcasts and special events. They also oversee all arrangements for affiliate interconnections. Today, the latter has become a maze of landlines, microwave links, and communications satellite systems. Usually, each affiliate presents its own special technical problems, and operations people have the job of solving them — all within a reasonable budget.

A network, like a station, depends upon the competence, creativity, and experience of its staff. The production and distribution of programming and the sales efforts of a network require the talents of producers, directors, announcers, a wide variety of on-air performers, technical personnel, sales and support people, and a myriad of other professional broadcast specialists. Most of these positions are filled by people who have had the benefit of extensive experience acquired by working in local radio stations. The talent, dedication, and efforts of a staff must come together as a unit under enlightened management for the network to reach its potential.

A few short years ago, a career in network radio was nothing more than a dream for many broadcast professionals. Today, such a career is within the grasp of many. Network radio lives. New and fresh concepts have evolved, and more are on the way. Your future and that of network radio are unlimited.

Chapter Eleven

Making It In Radio

Now that you have an understanding of the field of commercial radio, the wide range of careers it offers, and the ways in which stations and networks operate, you are in a better position to give some thought to your future in broadcasting. First, consider whether a career in radio is for you. If so, try to identify the areas within the industry for which your talents, temperament, and background are best suited. The jobs you *want* to do may vary considerably from the jobs you *can* do.

Before you make any decisions about a career in radio, you should learn as much as possible about what the business is really like. And those involved on a daily basis inside the industry are the best sources of this type of information. It would be most enlightening if you could meet personally with a number of successful broadcasters and discuss your future with each of them. But interviews of this type are probably not available to you. Instead, I have acted as your surrogate and posed the following questions to 19 outstanding professionals presently working in broadcast programming, sales, engineering, management, and education:

> Assume a person you do *not* know told you he or she wants a career in commercial radio. State what you recommend this person should do to:
> (1) determine if radio is for him or her,
> (2) prepare for a career in the field,
> (3) break into radio, and
> (4) advance within the industry.

The following responses represent a wide spectrum of candid opinion, helpful instruction, and straight talk from eminently qualified individuals. They are a cross section of the high caliber of talent that has made commercial radio the dynamic force it is today. Their thoughtful comments, based on many years of experience and a vast knowledge of broadcasting, provide you with rare insights about the field — what it offers and what it demands.

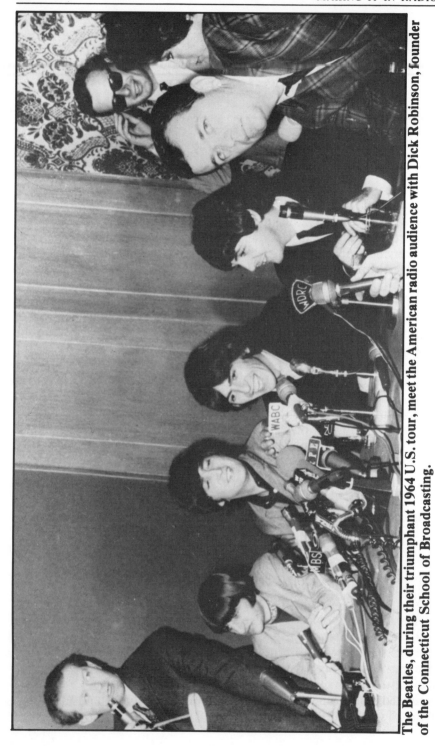

The Beatles, during their triumphant 1964 U.S. tour, meet the American radio audience with Dick Robinson, founder of the Connecticut School of Broadcasting.

JERRY BISHOP, FREELANCE ANNOUNCER AND MORNING MAN, KGIL RADIO, SAN FERNANDO, CALIFORNIA

So you want to get into radio. You are not alone. Throughout my 26 years as an on-air personality, hardly a week has gone by without at least one phone call from an inquiring, aspiring star broadcaster. Let's face it. Radio *is* an exciting, glamorous, and rewarding profession. But in this business, you get nothing for nothing. To enjoy a great career in radio — and reap the benefits, you must be disciplined, responsible, prepared to learn, and, most important, ready for some very hard work.

Before you dive headlong into any career field, you have to determine if it's for you. Radio offers quite a variety of jobs, each of which is important in the operation of a station, network, or any other broadcast organization. Naturally, my perspective is from the programming side. Your niche may be in sales, engineering, or administration. Remember, there are many interesting, challenging, and lucrative positions in the industry that you probably don't know exist. Investigate all of the career possibilities before you take the plunge.

Prior to making any decisions about a specific career or job, get a good, general education — especially in the three R's. Thereafter, I recommend that you take some basic broadcasting courses in college and visit radio stations as often as possible so that you acquire knowledge of broadcasting.

Let's suppose that you have done your homework and, after a general review of the positions available in radio, have come to the conclusion that on-air performing is for you. At this point, you should consider investigating the various schools of broadcasting in your area. A reputable operation will provide you with an opportunity to become familiar with the equipment of a radio station and to gain some instruction in announcing techniques which would not be available to you elsewhere. High school, college, and educational radio stations also afford great opportunities to gain experience in this field quickly.

One final, but very important thought. Don't restrict your radio performing to one area. Being a disc jockey is a great way to start and a lot of fun, but what do you plan to do after you hit 30? Work at becoming a well rounded on-air specialist in many areas. Prepare yourself for any eventuality. Your first job will probably be at a small station in a small market. Should this be the case, you'll have an outstanding opportunity to do everything at the station from interviews, news, sports, and mopping the studio floor. It will be a great adventure, and you'll love it. With hard work, experience, and a certain degree of luck, you will move on to bigger and better things in the field.

Radio has been extremely good to me. I hope it treats you as well.

BOB CAIN, ANCHORMAN, CABLE NEWS NETWORK

Anyone considering a career in broadcast journalism must prepare himself on what I call the *substantial* and *cosmetic* levels. In this context, "substantial" means the development of journalistic awareness and competence, and "cosmetic" signifies the performance aspects of the field.

A journalist in any medium is essentially a news factory. He must recognize and acquire raw materials, manufacture them into products, and deliver them to consumers. Facts and information from many sources are the newscaster's raw materials. After deciding what is "news," he writes stories which are his products. Broadcasts of those stories constitute delivery of the products to consumers, the audience.

Substantial preparation begins with the development of a great interest in human affairs. That interest must be fueled by the constant reading of good newspapers, news periodicals, journals, and books dealing with history, current events, and issues. Through this type of reading, one becomes comfortably conversant with the material he will be handling in interviews, while ad libbing, and in straight reporting. Adding to his store of personal knowledge is not merely part of the job — it must become a way of life.

One must first learn to read and write, and then to learn to read and write as a journalist. As a result, a major portion of substantial preparation is a college education. It is virtually a necessity, but a major in journalism is not. A four year period devoted exclusively to journalism would preempt valuable exposure to courses dealing with English, history, science, political science, philosophy, and other subjects. One learns journalism in his first few jobs, not in school. A few courses in writing for print or broadcast, however, are beneficial.

Much of the daily effort of a newsperson goes into writing. The only way to learn how to write is to write. There are no shortcuts. One must observe the methods used by good writers. Thereafter, he should produce his own stories and develop style. A few rules about news writing must be observed: First, a journalist must decide if a story is news or simply pap. The ability to tell the difference requires news judgment which is only acquired through experience. Producers and news directors give assistance in this area, but they are not gods. They make mistakes, but they've "been there" and are bound to know some things a novice does not. Secondly, the first draft of a story should never be considered acceptable. Copy should be reviewed and improved. It must be pared down, tightened up, and made more to the point. News writing should never be cute, but ought to be creative. Thirdly, wire copy should be questioned as to accuracy, grammar, and the overall treatment of the story. Finally, no matter what its source, a news story can always be improved.

The "cosmetic" aspect of broadcast journalism is its show business side. Like it or not, a newscaster is a performer. Most of us got into radio by sounding good and projecting credibility. Persons interested in broadcast journalism should listen to good on-air people, but ought not to imitate them. Each hopeful should try to figure out why the good ones are good and what they like about their deliveries. Thereafter, they should develop their own styles. This process *sounds* easier than it actually is. The criticism of friends and colleagues plus self-analysis is helpful in developing a novice's style. All of this is neither journalism nor the stuff of which Pulitzer prizes are made, but it is what is required to get that first job and succeed in this field.

JOHN G. CHANIN, VICE PRESIDENT - SPORTS
MUTUAL BROADCASTING SYSTEM

One of the questions most frequently asked of me by young candidates for broadcasting careers is, "Why do I have to take *(subject)* if I want to be a broadcaster?" The "subject" usually mentioned is a foreign language or a science or math course. One of the answers, of course, is to train the brain. Another is that exposure to a general, balanced curriculum teaches one how to study a program, think it out, analyze it, and recommend a solution. And still a third answer is to produce a well informed, diverse individual for an employer in an extremely competitive business in an extremely competitive world. Corporations are requesting, if not demanding, that employees be capable of contributing their time and talents to areas that are beyond their specialities.

It is important to attend an established college or university offering a four year program toward a degree in communications and/or broadcasting. It is equally important that the school have a working radio or television facility at which the student can actively work in as many job functions as is possible during four years. Load up on broadcasting and related courses, but don't ignore those dealing with foreign languages, math, science, advertising, sales, and marketing.

I know a few young people who majored in broadcasting/communications as undergraduates, went on to achieve a masters degree in business, and thereafter obtained law degrees as well. They are certainly exceptions, but, at 28 years of age, they hold exceptional, high salaried positions at the network level.

The job candidate who has worked in broadcasting or in broadcast related activities while a collegian should have an advantage obtaining a full-time position once acquiring the degree(s) because of the contacts made and the experience acquired. But, in any case, as the candidate attempts to find a position at the network level or at a station in one of the top ten markets, the search will be harsh. Employers in those strata demand experienced people, so plan to search elsewhere.

There are more than 8,000 commercial radio stations and 1,100 authorized television stations in the United States. Add to those numbers the mushrooming cable systems and other tangent businesses, and you have a pretty healthy training ground for jobs if you are willing to "pay the dues" in the "boonies." A planned, five year "staircase" will usually prepare the candidate for a position in broadcasting paying an above average salary.

A young person striving for executive management positions would do well to sprinkle a number of business, finance, sales, and marketing courses among his college curriculum. And, it would be wise to seek positions within sales, sales service, station relations, research, and advertising and promotion departments during his growth years to prepare a strong foundation for that top management post. Virtually every company or division president I served during the past quarter-century emerged from sales. Two were attorneys.

The challenge is there for the taking. The refreshing way to conquer it is through honesty and hard work. The rewards are many.

DON CHEVRIER, SPORTSCASTER, ABC RADIO AND TELEVISION NETWORKS AND THE TORONTO BLUE JAYS, THE AMERICAN LEAGUE, MAJOR LEAGUE BASEBALL

You have plenty of time to become a sportscaster. First, learn how to write. This may come as a jolt to aspiring young broadcasters in the sports field, but writing is an integral part of all aspects of this business. Writing even plays an important role in play-by-play work because you are actually creating a story through ad libs as you go. A pleasant speaking voice and a quick mind are gifts of birth, but writing well for broadcasting is an acquired skill.

To qualify for the position of sportscaster in local or national radio, you must learn both to write and to read well. The trend in the industry is to hire only those persons who can perform the dual functions of writing and announcing. Anyone in this field should seek to achieve the capacity to express himself in a clear, crisp, concise, and interesting way. A broadcast reporter usually has but one chance to make himself understood by his audience. A listener has no opportunity to review a cumbersome passage if he doesn't catch its meaning when broadcast. And a surefire way to give your thoughts definite form is to spread them on paper first.

A sportscaster must recognize that vast differences exist between writing and speaking styles. He has to develop the ability to write his thoughts down in a form that conveys his meaning in a style that is easily understood. Although the words are being read from a script, the listener should have the feeling that he is listening to a reporter *talking*, not reading.

Development of the "writing for radio" skill need not wait for your formal training to begin or your entry into the field of broadcasting. Listen to the various sportscasters heard in your area and analyze their styles. Thereafter, after attending sporting events or reading about them in your local newspaper, try to construct your own sportscast based on those stories. Then use a small tape recorder and read the sportscast as if you were going on the air. This type of home study program is an excellent start toward the development of your own style of both writing and announcing sports.

The field of sportscasting is by no means a Monday through Friday 9-to-5 world. But if you have the natural ability, possess the desire to learn, and are willing to keep plugging, it offers a stimulating, challenging, and rewarding career. Good luck.

BOB CRAIG, PROGRAM DIRECTOR, WMGK (FM), PHILADELPHIA

Starting out in radio is akin to embarking on a journey. You can take any number of routes to get to your destination, but it takes careful planning to choose the best way for you to go. To determine his options, the traveler looks first at a road map. Your options in the field of commercial radio broadcasting are usually on display at a local station in your home town.

If you're thinking about a career in radio, I recommend that you listen carefully to the widest variety of radio formats on the air in your area. The station whose music, announcers, news, promotion, and production appeal to you most is bound to be the best place for you to examine first. Contact that station's program or promotion director, explain your career goals and interests, and listen to the advice he gives you.

If radio is genuinely in your blood, you'll know it after spending some time around a station. Should you be attending a school that has its own station, you undoubtedly have acquainted yourself with its method of operation. Don't be confused. There is a world of difference between the workings of a typical college station and that of a business called a commercial radio station.

I have encountered quite a number of college students who have had the good fortune of spending substantial periods of time at a commercial station observing its operation and helping out as interns. They actually receive college credits for completing intern periods as part of their curricula. Their exposure to this type of environment is unbeatable. They are participating directly in commercial broadcasting. To be involved in the actual process is the ultimate experience for a novice.

If you are unable to attend a school that has its own station, the next best route to a career in radio is a course in a reputable school of broadcasting. Before enrolling in any such school, try to learn as much as possible about broadcasting. Be sure to visit a commercial radio station first before making a commitment to a career in this business. You must be positive that this field is for you. Be ready to eat, sleep, and drink radio. It is a tough and competitive field, and initially it offers little glamour or financial reward. If, however, you are willing to work very hard and have natural talent and a love for it, commercial radio offers unlimited opportunities.

As you acquire more experience within the field, your abilities are expanded, and you are capable of addressing greater challenges. There is always a decided shortage of unique on-air personalities and well rounded program directors. Once you've landed that first job, develop in as many areas of broadcasting as you can. The right combination of talent, desire, and acquired abilities will take you to the top.

PETER S. CRAWFORD, VICE PRESIDENT AND STATION MANAGER, WHDH, BOSTON

A station manager of a major market radio station is responsible for every aspect of its operation. And none is more important than sales.

Each week, I meet, on average, with two to three people who are seeking sales positions in radio. They are recent college graduates who want to break into the field, sales veterans hoping to move over from other stations or media, and individuals, experienced in other fields, hoping to make career changes. I make it a point to know who is working in radio sales in my market whether or not I have an opening. In that way, I know who is available when a slot needs to be filled at my station.

Good sales people in any field are few and far between. They are particularly hard to find in radio — and this should come as no surprise, given the lack of any available training in broadcast sales other than that acquired on the job. Engineers attend technical schools, and on-air performers get instruction through college speech and drama courses and schools of broadcasting. But the salesperson must learn by selling.

Anyone who has never sold radio should spend a couple of years in sales at a suburban station to find out if he or she likes selling. Basic training in radio sales is available there that major market stations neither have the time nor capacity to provide. These stations provide individuals with opportunities to be schooled in every facet of the business, not only sales. They write copy, produce spots, and do much more. Most important, they develop the techniques required to deal with all types of advertisers, especially those who have never used radio.

Most junior salespersons start their careers in radio by approaching retail businesses which traditionally rely more on print media. To sell effectively in this area, they must learn the methods used to attract business from other media, and to do so, they must know the strengths and weaknesses of *all* media, not just radio. Thereafter, through developing credible copy, preparing demonstration tapes, and producing good results, they soon win converts to radio.

It is apparent that good, solid small market experience is absolutely critical to succeed in radio sales. Most of all of the people in major market radio sales today started in smaller markets. That's where they got their feet wet, and that's where the washout rate is tremendous. People soon learn whether or not this end of the business is for them. If you can make it in sales in the small market, you can make it anywhere.

DONA S. GOODMAN, ACCOUNT EXECUTIVE, WPLR/WSCR, NEW HAVEN

Opportunities for women in radio sales have never been better or easier to find. Converting an opportunity into a career in this field, however, takes hard work, perseverance, and a love of the business. But if you can sell, life can be beautiful.

While enhancing your entire life, a college education qualifies you for a broader spectrum of careers. Such training is not always required in securing an entry level position in radio, but it is critical for advancement into management.

To sell radio effectively, you must know as much as possible about the business. In your first few jobs as an account executive, you spend as much time selling radio in general as you do in selling your own station. Time spent at a college or public station may give you excellent experience in programming and engineering, and the exposure is good. But the real business of commercial radio is business, and business means sales.

The best way to learn about commercial radio and the ways a station operates is through volunteer work. I recommend that you contact the manager of a local station and offer your services, explaining that it will cost him nothing. If you succeed in selling the idea, you will land a spot as an intern. Should you be attending college, check to see if your school grants credits for internships in this type of industry.

Once at work in a station, you should spend as much time as possible with people in *all* of its departments. An effective account executive must do more than sell. The sale is actually just the beginning of a chain of events in a long process. You soon discover that an account executive deals with advertisers and ad agencies, writes copy, and even serves as a bill collector. You do what is necessary to shepherd a buy through the cycle which runs from the actual selling of the time through the follow-up after the advertiser pays.

Throughout the entire period of your internship, ask questions and observe all of the activities. In an unobtrusive way, you should also learn about the negatives as well as the positives about sales from those who are actually in the field. People in this business are helpful, candid, and usually fun to work with. But after this whole intern process, you may even decide that radio is not for you.

Whether you start out as an intern or move right into a training program that is part of your first job, you soon learn that selling is very hard work. But success in sales leads to greater things. Most station executives come from the ranks in sales. And this should come as no surprise. To succeed in sales, you must be a secure individual who can cope with constant rejection. You must relentlessly press on and maintain high standards of integrity. Never promise anything you can not deliver.

Training programs in sales vary from station to station. If your first station's sales program is inadequate, I recommend that you consider investing in some of the commercial sales training courses available. You are constantly competing in this field with other stations and all of the other media, including print and television. It is no place for the inexperienced, unequipped, and uninformed.

Nailing down that first job and scoring some initial successes in sales do not signal the end of your learning process. It is continuous. There are always new techniques and approaches to discover and master. Radio is synonymous with change, and the effective account executive must stay ahead of the game. Your efforts are designed to solve problems through radio advertising. To do so, you must be committed to an unending study of people, their problems, and lifestyles.

DON IMUS, MORNING MAN,
WNBC RADIO, NEW YORK

If you are thinking about getting into radio, I recommend that you go to a local station and find out what people do there. Look at everything — sales, on-air performing, engineering, management — the whole operation.

Most people who ask me about radio want to be disc jockeys or comedy writers. No matter what you want to do in the field, go to college first and learn to speak and write English correctly. I believe that it is really important that you learn to express yourself properly. When you've got that down, get involved in a radio situation — one where you can learn the trade.

A college station is a great place to get some practical experience. Many are run in a professional manner and have standards and equipment that are as good as commercial stations. Prepare yourself to do a job at a commercial station and then go for it.

Radio is set up much like baseball. Its structure consists of the minor leagues and the major leagues. You must be prepared to start your career in outlying areas if you expect to acquire know-how and savvy about the business. To get into and *stay* in the major markets, you have to know your stuff. After attending college and a school of broadcasting, I started out in radio at a station in a town of 5,000 people and moved on to larger markets.

Many people also ask me how do you get to be funny on the air? You really have to be the same person on the air as off. You are what you are, and your listeners know exactly what that is. They can practically see you through the microphone. If you are a truly funny person, you can become a believably funny disc jockey. Just be yourself — and a little nuts!

Finally, learn how to encourage and develop good working relationships with the people with whom you work. Most things in radio —and life — are team efforts. You can't make it alone. A broadcast team works best when its members share mutual respect.

CHUCK KAITON, PLAY-BY-PLAY MAN
OF THE HARTFORD WHALERS OF THE
NATIONAL HOCKEY LEAGUE

I am privileged to be a major league play-by-play man. Most listeners are fooled by the ease by which announcers in my field perform. But it is demanding and pressurized work which requires great concentration under generally adverse conditions. Fortunately, it is also professionally gratifying and the most fun in sports besides actually playing in the game.

Play-by-play reporting is the *impromptu description* of a sporting event, with analysis, as it happens. It is impromptu because the description of a contest simply can't be rehearsed. No one knows what will happen. In radio, through his descriptions, the announcer paints a word picture of his view and perception of the events on the field of play for the listener.

A play-by-play man must possess certain attributes — some natural, others acquired — in order to create accurate and colorful descriptions. A good voice is a gift with which one is born. But the abilities to sound authoritative and convey excitement through a rapid fire delivery can be learned and developed through practice. He must have the common sense to decide in a fraction of a second precisely what is important and what need not be described. He must, therefore, have a perception of an event that is much wider than that of the average fan. A great deal happens away from the main flow of play in practically every game. Descriptions of these side activities add an important dimension to the involvement of the listener in the contest. For example, a hockey announcer must be aware of the action in all of the little areas of the ice. Most fans in the rink follow the puck, but he must report when things start to get a bit dicey in the corners. He actually anticipates penalty calls and each pass of the puck.

This work requires more than just a voice, the ability to describe, and a perception of the event. One must be a student of every aspect of the sport being described — rules, history, players, standings, etc. Also, a sportscaster should be able to operate the equipment in the booth at the scene. Today, he can not always count on having an engineer at his side.

How do you prepare for an exciting and rewarding career as a play-by-play announcer? There are numerous ways to get going, but I recommend the following:

1. Go to a college or university which has a student radio station active in sports broadcasting. Participation in its play-by-play programs is great experience. If you are unable to do so, take a tape recorder to sporting events and call them as if you were broadcasting live. In either case, criticize your work and develop a style of your own. Be

yourself, not an imitation of another broadcaster. Radio is a beautiful medium. It allows your personality to flow through to the audience. In this business, style plus personality equals success.

2. Volunteer your services to a local radio station. Pay is unimportant at the start of your career. Carry equipment, serve as a messenger, or work in the office. Do whatever will teach you about sports, news, and every other aspect of radio. Also, ask your favorite play-by-play broadcaster to allow you to sit in on a broadcast so that you can get an idea of what it takes to prepare and present a pre-game show, a play-by-play description, and intermission and post-game shows. I did this and was treated well by Tom Hedrick of the Texas Rangers and Dan Kelly of the St. Louis Blues.

3. After you have been working at announcing for a period of time, ask for appraisals of your work by professionals in the field. Most enjoy helping young people and appreciate being asked. It is very helpful to get some feedback from a pro about your work. Also, don't be afraid to send your tapes to radio stations for evaluations of your work by program directors.

Some people are simply not cut out to do play-by-play work. There are many other great and gratifying things to be done in radio. But if you feel you have the ability and personality, want to be an entertainer, and enjoy having fun, I encourage you to give play-by-play work a shot. There's a job out there for you if you are good enough to grab it.

DONNA RUSTIGIAN McCARTHY, ON-AIR PERSONALITY, WKRI, WEST WARWICK, RHODE ISLAND

They used to tell me that a woman's place in radio was in sales. And while this may have been true for most, I did not buy it. Rather, my instincts told me to pursue a personal goal of being an on-air performer. The decision was a good one, and, so far, I've had a wonderful experience.

To succeed in any aspect of the radio business, you must be informed, involved, and well-rounded. And this is really important in on-air positions. Although there are theatrical aspects to this role, you have to know a little about everything. The best preparation for this job is college. There, you should learn how to learn. If college is not for you or is beyond your means, learn to learn by yourself. Become a compulsive reader of newspapers, history books, and nonfiction writings.

While in your preparatory period, absorb as much as possible about the radio business by working at your school's radio station or interning at a local commercial or public station. I attended a school of broadcasting which provided me with some excellent experience and background in radio. It also assisted me in obtaining my first job.

Learning to be an on-air performer is not, however, a spectator sport. My first job consisted of an overnight shift at a small station. I learned more by working throughout the night alone in one week than during any other period of my life. I did a little bit of everything, including running the board, reading the news, playing music, and doing sports reports. The station's program director regularly reviewed my efforts and provided me with the type of guidance a novice needs to get a career going in the right direction. If such criticism is not available to you, you should listen to tapes of your own work and compare it with the on-air professionals you admire.

I recommend that if you have confidence in your ability and have prepared yourself sufficiently to qualify, get an on-air job as quickly as possible, and jump right in. You surely will make mistakes, but you will learn — and quickly. If you start off at a big station, management expects you to know everything. But at smaller stations, most people on the staff will be supportive and show you the way.

The approach an on-air performer uses on the air is determined mostly by the station's format and the targeted audience it seeks to attract. I try to be a good communicator, not an actress. The formats in which I have worked have allowed me to be myself on the air. Listeners and associates have told me that I act the same in person as I do on the radio. I make it clear that I do not act — I *am* myself on the air.

BYRON N. McCLANAHAN, VICE PRESIDENT AND GENERAL MANAGER, WKND RADIO, HARTFORD

I encourage all qualified people to get into the business of commercial radio. I really have positive feelings about its future. In my experience, there has never been a dull moment, and that makes it very rewarding. If you are a member of a minority group, however, the news about your prospects in the field is both good and bad. The good outweighs the bad.

A minority person is usually defined as a member of a racial, national, religious, or other group regarded as different from the larger group of which it is a part. From its beginnings, commercial radio has always considered minorities "different." Much has been written about the great opportunities now available to minorities in the field. Without doubt, some progress has been made since the late 1960's, but from this minority person's perspective, minority ownership of broadcast properties has increased very little and the proportion of minorities employed in the industry is unimpressive.

Minorities should not, however, be discouraged by the low number of representatives of their groups presently working in the industry. National exposure of the issue of minority involvement will eventually create a broader perspective of the question and produce the realization that minorities and commercial radio need each other to make it. Don't let the present industry conditions cause you to withdraw into a limited professional environment. I have found that minorities often isolate themselves in a predominately white or minority environment. You should concentrate on diversity. Careers often rise and fall quickly in commercial radio, so you must be able to adjust and grow at a fast pace as the world changes.

It is common for professionals in radio to advise young people that the only limitations they face in the industry are their own lack of drive or talent. With respect to minorities, this is simply not true. Many things about commercial radio are very "fraternal." The ranks of the industry have been pierced by minorities to a limited degree. For example, about 68 Blacks own approximately 138 of the more than 8,000 commercial radio stations in the United States. Fraternal structures are clearly counterproductive. The key to the success of minorities in this business is diversity of experience in *all* types of environments — white and minority. If you participate in any type of professional isolation, you will be the loser. There is no reason why some type of balance might not be achieved, and that balance results in communication among all sorts of people within the industry.

Generally speaking, minorities between the ages of 16 and 25 face more decisions than whites in determining their careers. They have to consider what areas are suited to their abilities. They also must painfully select those areas that are available to them, because not all are. When young minorities, hoping to break into the field, perceive the lack of other minorities in the industry, all sorts of things go through their minds as to what this industry is all about. Do not be discouraged. The minority population is clearly the fastest growing in this country, and strong, aggressive minority broadcasters can make tremendous contributions while experiencing unprecedented growth!

CHARLIE PARKER, VICE PRESIDENT AND
PROGRAM DIRECTOR, WDRC AM/FM, HARTFORD

There's far more to radio than meets the ear. One who wants to go into the field should first become acquainted with precisely what "radio" is. Most who express avid interest in broadcasting are enamored by its performance or "behind the mike" aspects as opposed to its "behind the scenes" opportunities. For one who has the aptitude and trainable potential to achieve the goal of being an on-air performer, this is all well and good. But it must be noted that the half dozen or so voices heard over the air on any given station represent a small part of its staff. All performers are supported by writers, producers, time salesmen, traffic controllers, programmers, music directors, engineers, and others who make up the bulk of the staff.

One need not close the door on the unique and rewarding careers in broadcasting if he is not qualified for a seat behind the microphone. One job usually leads to another in the same radio station or within the industry, and no one knows where a career in this field will lead. If one listens and learns on one job, he usually discovers and develops skills and aptitudes he may not have previously realized he possessed. Even an on-air performer may ultimately find greater fulfillment in an "off-air" position.

The composition of the staff of a radio station depends upon its size and sophistication. A tour of a station of some stature will, therefore, certainly be beneficial for the aspirant. If he is a young person, I recommend that an appointment for such a tour be made by a parent with a station's general manager, program director, or operation's manager. The broadcast executive should be advised of the purpose of the tour so that the hopeful gets more than a mere overview of the physical plant of the station. What should be stressed is the need for a comprehensive explanation of the various jobs. A high school graduate who makes his own appointment should also state that his purpose is occupational. And the key to getting the most out of the tour is the asking of all of the questions that come to mind.

Most radio stations are very cooperative in high school and college internship programs. The participating students observe the day-to-day functions of each department of a station. This arrangement is not only a fascinating experience, but it also provides vital information on which career diversions may be made. Nothing can match actually watching a deejay do a show, seeing a reporter prepare his newscast, or observing a producer as he creates and records a commercial.

Some high schools and many colleges have their own radio stations. They offer invaluable "hands on" experience to the student who takes radio seriously in spite of the prevalence of some purposeless staffers. Participation in high school and college drama groups can also

enhance one's versatility. In all of these activities, each student's moti-
vation and determination are the keys to the benefit he derives.

A reputable school of broadcasting can serve a worthwhile purpose
in terms of securing a position for the novice in radio. But such a school
is no better than the beginner's potential and aptitude. Acceptance by
and graduation from a broadcasting school should not be regarded as a
guarantee of subsequent employment in radio.

RON PELL, VICE PRESIDENT AND GENERAL SALES MANAGER, BUCKLEY BROADCASTING CORPORATION OF CONNECTICUT — WDRC AM AND FM

I recommend that any prospective candidate for a career in radio, especially in sales, gain some experience in his area of specialization, whether within or without the field. In addition, he should acquire a general background in all phases of the industry. I had several years of sales experience outside of the field. Once I got into commercial radio and gained the necessary knowledge of its product, I achieved success quickly.

The main task for a candidate in radio sales is the gaining of actual sales experience. If you are presently in school, take as many courses related to sales as possible. Marketing, merchandising, and business courses generally are very helpful. Once out of school, it is imperative that you gain some actual sales experience in the market place. The most helpful experience is that which is geared to consumer or retail selling since this is the type of selling you will be assigned at the start of your sales career in commercial radio. Before I got into radio, I sold a varied line of chemical products, business machines, medical instruments, and advertising. Armed with this experience, I easily landed my first job in radio. When I began as a sales representative at a radio station, I was determined to learn all aspects of the business so that in making sales calls, I could quickly establish a productive list of accounts. After one year of experience in a suburban AM station, I was able to graduate to an AM/FM combination and adopt to a larger market environment.

In order to sell, a sales representative must have a thorough knowledge of the workings of a radio station. There is more to sales than selling. After the order has been taken from an advertiser, the sales representative is responsible to make sure that the order is properly executed. He is involved with everything including copywriting, studio production, trafficking (the actual scheduling of the "spots" on the program log), and the billing on the completion of the schedule.

But "a general background in all phases of the industry" means much more than an understanding of the workings of a radio station. A radio sales representative must have a working knowledge of advertising agencies, the media that compete with radio, the characteristics of his market, and all aspects of the business.

A winner in this field never stops learning. Once you've decided on a career in broadcast sales, get the experience, acquire some knowledge, and then do the most important thing of all in order to insure success —work hard!

JIM PERRY, CHIEF ENGINEER, WKSS (FM), HARTFORD

Radio engineering is basically the installation, operation, and repair of an endless array of amazing pieces of electronic and mechanical equipment. Although many routes lead to a rewarding career in this field, each candidate's journey usually starts at an early age with a fascination for gadgets of all types and descriptions.

Many of today's engineers, in response to their interests in technical matters, became amateur radio operators while still in grade school. Through this approach, as young people, they gained solid, basic knowledge of electronics which became "second nature" well before they had to make decisions about higher education. Some began more obscurely as general tinkerers or audiophiles with passion for equipment. Still others began as computer buffs with soft spots for hardware. Even aspiring disc jockeys, who subconsciously desired to work with some of the machinery of radio, have become successful broadcast engineers.

My recent, informal survey of several engineers revealed that the two most frequently used methods to start careers in this area of broadcasting are (1) the "earn as you learn" or the "seat of your pants" method, and (2) formal higher education. The first method usually works as follows: a chronic tinkerer or ham radio operator lands a job right out of high school at a local radio station. He probably approached the station during a moment of need which is almost *any* time for small stations. It needed a body, and the budding engineer began "hands on" training. If he is fortunate, he may have the tutelage of an experienced supervisor. Should the station not have a regular engineer, he is on his own from the start. Landing such a job on bravado rather than basic engineering knowledge can be a frightening experience. As chaotic as this approach sounds, it is surprisingly prevalent. But it takes a special kind of person with natural talent and a positive, self-starting attitude to succeed using this haphazard method.

The second method, if carefully planned, is the ideal combination of on the job training and formal higher education. A student, using this approach, selects a technical school or engineering college which has its own campus radio station. The formal education and the work within the station provide him with technical knowledge and actual experience. A variation of this method occurs when a student chooses to attend a school near a good size radio or television market and obtains part-time work at a public or commercial station either as an employee or a volunteer. Most stations welcome volunteers with open arms. This method is preferred since the lucrative broadcast engineering jobs, especially in large stations, are filled by candidates who possess both a degree in electrical engineering and several years of experience on the local level.

Radio, television, and allied fields, such as cable, audio-video production, and satellite communications, are constantly evolving. The engineers responsible for the equipment that makes all of that possible enjoy jobs and lives that are vital, rewarding, and fascinating.

WILLIAM F. RASMUSSEN, VICE PRESIDENT, SATELLITE SYNDICATED SYSTEMS, INC. AND FOUNDER OF ESPN CABLE NETWORK

So you want to get into radio — that's great! You could not have picked a better time. Radio in the United States is presently on the threshold of its most dynamic period since The Golden Age of Radio — the satellite era.

Throughout its exciting, innovative history, commercial radio has succeeded by meeting all types of competition. It has confronted the challenges of newspapers, magazines, television, and cable by developing unique services, creating new markets, and utilizing advanced technology.

As you start out as a novice in commercial radio, plan your future in a way that takes advantage of the emerging technology used in the industry. Through solid preparation and "laboring in the vineyards," you have the ability right now to become part of radio's wonderful future.

In the beginning, you should learn the business — and it is a business — from the ground up at a radio station in a small to medium size market. Take any job that's available. Your initial objective is to become well schooled in the fundamentals of the industry. Your preconceived notions about the glamourous side of radio will probably result in frustrations, but this too shall pass. And throughout this entire period, learn, read, and observe about all aspects of the business.

After you have gained some basic experience in the field, you should make a determination as to precisely what area of specialization within radio is for you. Be it engineering, sales, or programming, make your choice and go after a job in that area with verve, tenacity, and imagination. Thereafter, no matter what your area of specialization, continue the learning process so that some day you are prepared sufficiently to move into the ranks of broadcast management. And radio has served as the springboard for careers in many other fields. Staffs in television, advertising, public relations, and technical equipment manufacturing, just to mention a few, abound with old radio hands.

I am an unwavering believer in the opportunities available to us simply because we live in America. And commercial radio is as American as you can get. In this great country, you *can* be what you choose to be. Your possibilities for success in radio are bound only by the limits of your own imagination.

DICK ROBINSON, FOUNDER AND PRESIDENT OF THE CONNECTICUT SCHOOL OF BROADCASTING, FARMINGTON AND STRATFORD, CONNECTICUT

"Tell it like it is" has been the philosophy of The Connecticut School of Broadcasting ("CSB") since its establishment in 1965. Getting on the air as a professional in radio takes much more than just a good voice. The recipe for success in broadcasting consists of equal parts of training, talent, practice, ambition, and perseverance. But, analogous to the creation of a delectable souffle, in spite of the existence of all of the proper ingredients, without a dash of luck, there is no guarantee that the results of one's efforts will produce a successful career in this field.

The number of job openings in the industry continues to expand, but most of these positions are not being filled by novices. Radio stations and networks want people with backgrounds in the business. As a result, a foundation of knowledge of the industry and its complexities is usually necessary for one to land that first job.

There are a number of ways to break into radio. I would never discourage one from obtaining a college education. The possession of a degree, however, has little bearing on where one begins his career. With or without degrees, most hopefuls start out making very little money at small stations in suburban or rural locations.

Experience at a radio station is another worthwhile route to follow in the quest of the status of professional broadcaster. But, realistically, most stations are not equipped to instruct a beginner in the intricacies of the business. They neither have the time nor patience and are usually hesitant to work with an individual who has virtually no knowledge of the media.

Another approach is an occupational school such as CSB. We stress basics. In the coming years, more of the jobs in radio and television will be available to persons with specialty skills than with college degrees alone. At the outset of your career, it will be very beneficial for you to know as much as possible about all aspects of broadcasting. Our students "learn by doing" from radio and television professionals who work in announcing, newscasting, writing, production, writing copy, and sales. As in any field, the more you know, the more valuable you will be to a broadcast team.

Within a month or two after graduation, many CSB students land jobs in the field. They begin by making modest salaries in small to medium markets, but they get a start. The rest is up to them. They are equipped to grow within their jobs and move on to positions offering greater career rewards. Within a short period of time on the job, they *know* they have been bitten by the broadcasting bug. For the first times in their lives, they can't wait to wake up each day and go to work. From that point on, they are confirmed broadcasters for life.

PAULA E. SCHNEIDER, ACCOUNT EXECUTIVE, WNBC RADIO, NEW YORK

Many people are initially attracted to careers in radio by its show business aspects. Thereafter, some of them gravitate to sales when they realize programming is not for them and appreciate what this challenging area has to offer. Others are attracted directly to sales by the lure of the possible, immediate financial rewards their efforts can produce. It soon becomes apparent to most radio people that sales provides great opportunities to advance into the ranks of management. A majority of today's radio managers and executives made their first marks in sales.

Good sales people must be problem solvers. They should have the ability to recognize the needs of advertisers and possess the knowledge and experience to fill them. To succeed, they should have a broad understanding of retail and other businesses and a comprehensive knowledge of all aspects of radio. Station sales, programming, and engineering personnel must interact effectively if they are ever to function as a team.

If you are a high school student and are considering a career in radio sales, concentrate on the basics necessary to prepare yourself for college. Any radio experience you get along the way is invaluable. While I recommend college training, it should not be exclusively in the broadcasting area. The typical college broadcasting curriculum consists of courses in announcing, writing, production, etc. These all relate to the programming aspects of broadcasting, but do not provide a background in sales and management. On the other hand, courses such as marketing, accounting, sales, and management will provide you with an awareness of general business principles and the tools with which to compete.

A salesperson should have a thorough understanding of the businesses of the station's clients. As an account executive with a degree in business administration, you will be a much more creative professional and able to provide effective approaches for your advertisers. In addition, with such a degree, you are in a better position for promotions that lead directly into management.

While in college, you should intern at a local commercial station in as many different departments as possible while emphasizing sales. Attendance at sales meetings and making calls are also invaluable experiences. You should also develop a habit of reading trade publications to be aware of new techniques and methods of operations.

Your first job in sales is very important. You must be willing to take any assignment provided it will eventually lead to your goal of securing a position as an account executive. Before taking a job as a secretary, sales assistant, or promotion aid, you should be assured that it will provide you with an opportunity to move upward within the company. If a job at any level leads no place, pass it up.

You have to do much more than get good sales results to move from the position of account executive into one with management responsibilities. You must obtain excellent results at whatever you undertake and be highly organized in every effort. While you should be a good team player, it is essential that you are noticed by management. To do so, take on special projects that will showcase your managerial skills. Expand your own scope by getting to know all of the department heads of the station and finding out what they do. Continue to read trade journals. Carefully set short and long term goals and make sure that you tell the right people within the organization about your career objectives. Prove to them that you are going to get what you want and ask for their help to get it. And always listen to what they have to say. Constantly review and improve your results, work hard, and your future will be bright.

ELTON L. SPITZER, GENERAL MANAGER OF
WLIR (FM), GARDEN CITY, NEW YORK, AND
PRINCIPAL OWNER OF WLYF (FM), SOUTH BRISTOL
(ROCHESTER), NEW YORK

You don't start out in this business as the general manager of a commercial station. Call it what you will — paying your dues or laboring in the vineyards — you need radio experience and knowledge before you can be considered for a top spot in management.

The vast majority of general managers receive their training in sales. How do you break into sales? First, get your start at a radio station, and then concentrate on moving into sales. By demonstrating initiative, persevering, and maintaining the proper attitude, you can make it in radio.

Select a college that operates a good commercial radio station. Not all schools' stations are licensed to carry commercials. If yours doesn't or you do not plan to attend college, try to become an intern at a local station. You can accomplish this in many ways. Determine if a friend or relative is an advertiser or has some pull with a station or a general manager. Perhaps a professor or employer will recommend you. Contact every station in town on your own, and let them know you're available.

Build a good record at your college station or during your internship, and use it as leverage when trying to break in. Keep a file on each sales matter in which you participate. Your presentations, statistics, and contracts are evidence of your achievements and will go a long way toward obtaining your first full-time job in commercial sales.

You are at a decided advantage by seeking positions in sales. They pay well, and most young people shy away from the field because they do not understand it. Most are attracted by the apparent excitement and glamour of on-air positions. These jobs are the most sought after, but they pay the least.

Once working in a commercial station, try to acquire a working knowledge of every activity at the station, including programming, writing copy, production, engineering, promotion, and traffic, but always keep your eye on the primary target: sales. By knowing how each department of the station works, you will be a better equipped salesperson.

Your initiative will get you into positions to show what you can do, and results will demonstrate your perseverance. Throughout the entire process, your attitude is critical. Without a positive attitude, you will not be at any station very long. It has no time for anything less. You must believe that your success is possible and that you can make it happen.

As an intern, be a goffer. In this business, you never know where an honest effort will lead you. An actual case comes to mind. A young man I know attended college in the Boston area. He wanted to do sports, an area of radio that is very competitive. He gained excellent radio experience by doing everything at his college station. He got to know people in commercial radio and hounded them night and day for an internship. Finally, he was offered a position from midnight to 4 A.M., Friday night/Saturday morning, because nobody else wanted it. During one of his shifts, a big fire broke out and, being the only one available, he was sent out to cover the story. He arrived on the scene, filed an outstanding report, and when a position as producer of the station's sports talk show opened, he got it. Lucky? Maybe. But if he had not taken a menial job, had the correct attitude, and persevered, he would not have had the opportunity to show his stuff.

Try to get close to the salespersons at the station, but do not be overbearing. Get involved in all of the sales activities. Attend the sales meetings, volunteer to help during promotions, and don't be afraid to let them know what you want to do in the future. When you graduate, the people with whom you have worked will provide you with leads for jobs and will serve as references. Take any job that gets you into commercial radio, and then shine. Dollars are not your primary concern — getting a break is.

Initiative, perseverance, attitude and a dash of good luck, and you can make it to the top in radio.

WALT WHEELER, REPORTER, WCBS/NewsRadio 88, NEW YORK

"If you're not crazy about this business, you'd have to be crazy to stay in it."

Walt Wheeler, WCBS/New York
ca. 1970, '75, '80, '81, '82...

(Sorry, but as a reporter, you won't find very many situations where you're ALLOWED to quote yourself.)

And there is a serious answer in that apparently "flip" quote: It is, in theory, possible for a radio reporter to find glamour, excitement, or even wealth in this business.

In fact, it even happens... sometimes. Usually, the first two or even three times the average cub covers a parking ticket, she or he is apt to find, if not riches, at least excitement and glamour, in the very fact of "being out there, covering a story,"... ANY story.

But the fourth time, it palls. And by the umpteenth time... well, if you, the reader, become that reporter, you're going to need a better reason for staying in this business than fame or fortune provides for most of us.

So be sure you're an out and out ham, who can't live without the glory of it all; or someone who cares vitally and believes earnestly —even fanatically — that a democratic society can be only as good as its information; or else do yourself a favor, and pick an easier road to popular acclaim and great affluence — like say, street-sweeping.

Is anybody still here?

OK, then this is just for you, now that we've chased the crowd. Now, as to how to get ready for, into, and ahead in radio reporting — here's the secret formula in 9 easy rules:

1. Get yourself a sound liberal arts education: Broadcast journalists (to be more than just a little high-fallutin' about it) cover a broad range of stories and need a broad background to do that. Read — literature, politics, hard and "dismal" science, current events and ancient history. Write — as if your life depended on it. Talk — always aiming for that special kind of articulateness which is clear and concise, off the cuff.

2. Take any available opportunity to work in this business — as a volunteer, an intern, an underpaid part-timer (if you should be that lucky) — anywhere, anytime. Managers would rather hire somebody who's already "proven" his or her worth... and a lot of managers act as though the fact that somebody else hired you first amounts to the prerequisite "proof."

3. Listen... and then listen some more, to the way other people do this job. Most of them have something to teach you, and somewhere behind a speaker grille is the reporter whose way of doing things is going to seem to be a style that fits you.

But after you've begun to be able to imitate that reporter (and you will try — everyone does, despite the fact that for most people, doing so leads them into a dead end) — well, stop! Let your own distinctive "voice" develop instead.

4. As implied by 3, listen to yourself, too. Enjoy! Even glow at just how well you tell a story every now and again. But listen to the time you fail to tell a story well, too, and figure out why.

5. Learn to use sound ... playing back the sound of the wind howling across a mike as you talk about "that" storm belting "your town" may tell your listener as much as your words; the spontaneous (even if ungrammatical) epigram from somebody who cares about the "event" you're covering may illuminate it for that audience hiding inside your microphone or tape machine; the fatuous pomposity purporting to be political wisdom may say enough about a proposal or program than all the pro- and con- you could fit in your next five newscasts.

6. Grow sharp eyes, a nose, and elbows — the kind that help you spot or smell out the story that others miss, or help you get to it in a crowd.

7. Go the extra mile on every assignment, no matter how unpromising.

8. Be lucky! Also smart, quick, brave, clean and ... Master everything above before you even try to get lucky enough to get your first job, because once you land the first one, you've done the hard part. Well, one hard part, anyway.

9. Keep your feet dry, and never bypass a restroom ...

And, if you've persevered to this point, through the mixture of fact and foolishness above — Good Luck! Some of us who are still "crazy about this business" are going to be awfully happy to have you first join, and then replace us.

Due to many factors, opportunities for rewarding careers in radio have never been better. This favorable situation is, in part, the result of the basic philosophy of the FCC. Congress created the agency for the purpose of producing a larger and more effective use of radio in the public interest. In furtherance of that goal, the FCC has dedicated itself to the proposition that "more is better." Throughout its history, the FCC has done whatever is necesary to increase the number of radio outlets.

From 1935 to 1978, the FCC presided over a 13 fold increase in the number of commercial stations in the United States, and it is not through yet. It has continually considered and acted on proposals which made more frequency allocations available to prospective licensees. Illustrative of these proposals are (1) new restrictions on present clear channel stations, resulting in new stations in the AM band, and the conversion of some daytime stations to full-time operations; (2) the expansion of both the AM and FM spectra; and (3) utilization of new, lower power Class A-1 and Class B-1 FM stations.

Commercial factors are also increasing the number of opportunities in radio. Unlike any other medium, radio has the instant ability to react to the specific needs and tastes of local, regional, and national markets. These needs and tastes are constantly shifting. The great number of radio stations has caused dramatic developments in the types of formats being developed and utilized. The finer definitions of targeted audiences within each market have forced stations to be innovative in order to compete effectively. These factors and the new technology have insured radio's future.

Radio people have been called the eternal pioneers. They started broadcasting itself. They developed the ability to entertain, inform, and influence millions. They created the first truly local broadcasting service through specialized formats. Many changes are occurring in the industry, but change has been the very essence of radio from its beginning. Radio people are prepared for the future.

Breaking into radio will always be difficult. The competition is generally fierce because the job seekers continually outnumber the available positions. But opportunities are constantly opening as people move up to positions of higher responsibility within and without the industry. If you have talent, drive, a little bit of luck, and knowledge of the field, success is attainable. It's out there for the earning. Good luck!

GLOSSARY OF TERMS COMMONLY USED IN RADIO BROADCASTING

ABC — Owner and operator of radio and television networks and stations; American Broadcasting Company.

Account — An advertiser, a client.

Account Executive — Radio time salesperson.

Across-the-board — A program broadcast at the same time each day, usually 5, 6, or 7 times a week.

Actuality — A broadcast or recording at an event; no use of sound effects.

ADI or Area of Dominant Influence — A standard geographical area, composed of a number of counties, where the local stations dominate in total hours listened. It is used by various audience measurement services.

Adult Contemporary — A radio format.

Adjacencies — Commercial time immediately before or after a program.

Ad Lib — A statement or program that is not rehearsed or scripted; an improvisation.

Affidavit — A sworn statement certifying that certain commercials or announcements were broadcast at specific times.

Affiliate — A radio station which broadcasts the programming of a network.

AFM — A union of musicians; The American Federation of Musicians.

Afternoon Drive-time — The hours when workers are returning home from their places of employment, usually 3 P.M. to somewhere between 6 P.M. and 8 P.M., depending on the market.

Air Check — A recording of a part of a radio program or broadcast day for demonstration or analysis purposes.

Airman — Talent who performs on the air.

Airshift — The scheduled period of work of on-air talent.

Allocation — The assignment of a frequency at a specified power to a licensee by the FCC.

All News — A radio format.

AM or Amplitude Modulation — A method of transmitting radio waves at frequencies from 535 kHz to 1605 kHz. Also called the standard broadcast band.

Announcements — Commercial or public service messages of varying lengths, also called spots.

Antenna — The part of radio transmitting and receiving equipment which is used to propogate waves into the air or to receive transmitted waves.

AOR — A radio format; album oriented rock music, also called progressive.

Applicant — A person or firm applying to the FCC for something.

Arbitron or ARB — Arbitron Ratings Company; a commercial service which estimates the size, composition, and other aspects of radio audiences in markets throughout the United States. Its data is gathered in various methods including diaries completed by selected listeners.

ASCAP — A music licensing organization; The American Society of Composers, Artists, and Publishers.

Attenuation — Reduction in the level of program signal.

Audience Index — The hours in which a radio station best reaches its targeted audience.

Audio — Transmission, reception, or reproduction of sound.

Audition — A trial performance to test on-air performer, program material, or equipment.

Authorized Power — The power assigned to a station by the FCC.

Availabilities or Avails — Uncommitted time periods within the broadcast day where commercials might be placed.

Average Frequency — The average number of times the targeted audiences hears a commercial.

Average Quarter-Hour Persons or AQH — The average number of persons of any demographic group listening within an average quarter-hour.

Average Quarter-Hour Rating — The percentage of the population group listening at any time within a given quarter-hour, calculated by dividing the average quarter-hour persons by the population.

Background — The music or sound designed to create an environment or mood in front of which the main program content is highlighted.

Back-timing — The process where program segment is timed from the point it ends rather than from the beginning. Segment may start with no volume and be brought up in volume to end at a certain time.

Back-to-Back — Two or more announcements with no other programming between them.

Backtrack — Placing a stylus on album or recording and manually spinning it until sound on track is heard; cueing device.

Baffles — Materials used in broadcasting and recording studios to absorb sound to prevent one audio element from overcoming another.

Balance — The placement of microphones to obtain an acceptable sound which provides a high ratio of direct sound from indirect sound; the proper mixture of sounds to produce an acceptable result.

Barter — The trading of commercial time for goods or services rather than for money. Also, the providing of program material for availabilities for use by the provider rather than direct payment to provider.

Beautiful Music — A radio format, also called Good Music.

Bed — The instrumental background music of jingle or commercial.

Bidirectional Microphone — A microphone which picks up sound to its front and rear and rejects sound generated at its sides.

Billboard — An audio statement concerning a program or segment which is to be broadcast later.

Billing, Gross — The billing amount on which commissions for sales are computed.

Billing, Net — A non-commissionable billings amount.

Bird — A communications satellite.

Bird Feed — The transmission of programming by communications satellite.

Bit — A small part; a show business routine.

Black — A format directed at a black targeted audience.

Blend — A combination of sounds which mix properly.

Block — Segment of log or programming blocked out or reserved.

Block Programming — A grouping of programs of similar appeal.

Blow — The improper delivery of a program segment. An announcer's goof.

BMI — A music licensing organization; Broadcast Music Incorporated.

Board — An audio control panel or console.

Book — A rating report or survey.

Boom — An overhead microphone stand.

Bonus Spots — Free commercials given as a part of a paid schedule.

Booth — A small enclosed area from which an announcer works.

Brand — Identifying symbols used to distinguish a seller's goods and services from those of its competition; also used to create advertiser's image.

Break — See Station Break.

Break Up — An attack of laughter and giggles which prevents an on-air performer from continuing the regular course of his show. Also, an interruption in a radio signal.

Bridge — Sound or music used to span two separate scenes or situations on the air.

BTA — Availabilities with no specific time periods paid in fixed amounts by advertisers under an agreement with the station that its commercials shall be placed in the best time available. Also called run of schedule or ROS.

Build — An intensification of emotion by the increasing of tempo or volume through all types of program matter.

Bulletin — A special news announcement about an event or situation important enough to interrupt regular programming.

Buy — The purchase of commercials by advertiser or agency.

Buying By The Numbers — A purchase of commercial time made exclusively on the basis of rating surveys.

Call Letters — The identifying letters assigned to each radio station by the FCC. Also called call sign.

Canned — Recorded program matter, distinguished from a live performance.

Cans — Headphones or earphones.

Capstan — The drive spindle on a tape deck.

Card — A rate card which sets forth a radio station's current charges for commercial time.

Cardioid Microphone — A microphone with a heart shaped pickup pattern.

Cartridge — Also called cart, it is a plastic case holding a continuous loop of tape used for news, jingles, commercials, and records. Also, a container for a stylus which produces sound from a phonograph recording.

Cassette — A tape container narrower than a cartridge in which the tape is played from end to end and is not continuous.

CBS — Owner and operator of radio and television networks and stations; CBS Inc., formerly known as the Columbia Broadcasting System

Channel — (1) An AM or FM frequency on which a station is authorized to broadcast; (2) A track of multi-track tape; (3) Boards or consoles contain channels for input and output of program matter.

Circulation — The number of persons who receive a radio station or network during a particular time, usually a week or a month.

Citation — An FCC allegation of an infraction by a licensee.

City Grade Signal — The signal strength which must be produced throughout the geographical limits of a station's city or town of license per FCC regulations.

Classical — A radio format.

Clear Channel Station — An AM station, usually with 50,000 watts of power, on a frequency either unused by other stations or used by a very small number of other stations across the country.

Close — The closing or ending announcement of a program.

Cluster Buster — A noncommercial bit of programming used to separate closely spaced commercials.

Cold — A performance without rehearsal or planning.

Combination Rate — A reduced spot rate for using two stations (AM and FM) in one market.

Commentary — The presentation of opinion rather than fact.

Commercial — An announcement which advertises a product, service, or institution, also called a spot.

Commercial Impressions — Total number of persons exposed to a commercial message, counting each person each time exposed.

Commercial Manager — An executive in charge of a radio station's time sales and related areas.

Commercial Protection — The amount of time, per station policy, that must separate commercials for products and services of competitors.

Communications Satellite — A satellite in an orbit 22,300 miles above the equator, equipped with transponders and antennas, revolving at a rate of speed synchronous with the earth's rotation, giving the appearance that it is hovering over a fixed point on the earth's surface.

Community Survey — A study of the needs of the community served by a radio station.

Composite — An audio track containing several program elements.

Compressor — An automatic device that reduces the dynamic range of a signal to a desired level. Also called a limiter.

Condenser Microphone — A microphone which uses varying capacitants between two charged plates, a fixed base plate and a diaghram, to create an electrical signal. It is electrostatic rather than electromagnetic.

Console — A board used for the controlling and mixing of sound.

Construction Permit — FCC authorization to build new radio or television station; also called CP.

Contemporary Music — Loosely defined term which usually refers to the present, most popular music. Also, a synonym for rock music.

Continuity — Written links between segments broadcast which may include commercial copy, public service announcements, programs, and promotions.

Contour Lines — A station's signal coverage area as mathematically calculated and shown on a map.

Control Room — The production and operation area containing turntables, tape machines, boards, etc. where programs are mixed and monitored.

Cooperative Advertising — The combination of national and local or regional advertisers' messages into one commercial, the cost of which is shared by both. Also called coop.

Copy — News, sports, advertising, or public service scripts.

Cost Per Thousand or CPM — The actual cost of reaching one thousand persons by a given radio station. As an example, if a commercial costs $25.00 and 10,000 persons are listening, the CPM is $2.50.

Cough Button — A switch or button in a studio which cuts off a microphone to prevent the cough or throat clearing of talent from being broadcast.

Country — A radio format.

Coverage Area — The geographical area reached by the prime signal of a radio station as shown on coverage map. Also, the number of persons who can receive a radio station or network.

CP — Construction permit; FCC authorization to build radio or television station.

Cross Fade — A transition from one program source to another; the fading out of one as the other is being faded in.

Crosstalk — Interference from one circuit breaking into another.

Cue — The signal or indication to start a particular operation or announcement, usually given by hand or a cue light.

Cume or Cumulative Audience — The total number of different persons reached by a radio station's programming in a specified time period, such as a week or a month. Also, the station's net or unduplicated audience.

Cut — (1) Stop!; (2) A track on a sound recording; (3) To take out some program elements; (4) To record a spot. (5) To stop one program short and insert another such as a news bulletin.

Day-parts — The traditional division of the broadcast day into the following sections: Morning Drivetime - 6 A.M. to 10 A.M.; Daytime - 10 A.M. to 3 P.M.; Afternoon Drivetime - 3 P.M. to 7 P.M.; Evening - 7 P.M. to 12 Midnight; Overnight - 12 Midnight to 6 A.M.; Weekends.

Daytime — A day-part, usually 10 A.M. to 3 P.M. on weekdays.

Daytimer — An AM station authorized to broadcast only from local sunrise to local sunset.

Dead Air — The broadcast of nothing. A silent gap in programming.

Dead Spots — Areas within a radio station's coverage where its signal is weak or nonexistent due to its directional array or local topographical conditions.

Decibel or DB — A unit for measuring the intensity of sound on a scale from zero for no sound to 130 for sound that causes pain in human beings.

Deejay — Disc jockey; D.J.

Degausser — A unit which erases audio tapes by demagnetizing them.

Demodulator — A part of a downlink that receives specific signals being transmitted by a communications satellite.

Demographic Share — The percentage of all the listeners of a station or network that fall into a specific demographic group during a particular time period.

Demographics   Statistics used in broadcasting that divide the population in a given market into groups by age, sex, education, income, etc.

DGA — A guild representing radio, television, and film director; Directors Guild of America.

Dial Position — The place on the AM or FM dial where a given station is found.

Diary — A special type of questionnaire used to measure a person's or family's radio listening activity in one week for rating purposes.

Directional Signal — A radio signal which is more powerful in some directions than in others. It is created by an impulse with a pattern other than circular in shape, generally used to protect other radio stations from interference or to increase coverage to a particular area.

Direct Response Ads — Advertising copy designed to cause listeners to respond by telephone or mail directly to the advertiser. It contains the telephone number or address of the advertiser.

Director — An individual who supervises the production of a program or commercial.

Distortion — An inaccurate reproduction of a signal caused by change in the frequency of the output wave. Also, a measurement of the combined radio harmonics of the audio frequency range.

Documentary — An extended news program which examines a particular problem or aspect of society.

Dolby — An electronic noise reduction system used to produce sound of the highest possible fidelity in the transmission and reception of FM signals and in the recording of sound.

Donut or Doughnut — A commercial composed of live copy inserted between a recorded opening and closing. Also called a sandwich.

Down and Under — The lowering of the audio level of sound effects or music while copy is delivered over it as a background.

Downlink — An earth receiving station, consisting of a dish type antenna or large parabolic reflector, used to take down satellite signals.

Drivetime — Morning and afternoon time periods when a large number of listeners are driving to and from work. Times vary by markets, but 6 A.M. to 10 A.M. and 3 P.M. to 7 P.M. are typical.

Dropout — A spot on a magnetic tape recording where a loss of signal caused by a faulty tape or poor splice occurs.

Dub or Dubbing — The transfer of program material from one tape to another. A tape copy or the copying of a tape.

Earphones — A device placed on or in ears, used when other program elements must be heard by on-air personality but not picked up by live microphone. Also used to communicate with on-air performer. Called cans, headphones, or headset.

Earth Station — A general term that refers to both communications satellite uplinks and downlinks.

Echo — A repetition of sound produced by the reflection of sound. May be produced electronically or by an echo chamber to add presence to live broadcasts.

Echo Chamber — A room constructed in a way to produce sound with an echo effect.

Editing — Removal, addition, and rearrangement of taped program material, usually to fit a specific time period, performed by cutting the tape with a blade and splicing it with special adhesive tape or by dubbing.

Effects Microphone — A microphone placed at live special events to pick up background sounds to be mixed with the main program source.

Electrical Transcription — An old-time radio term for a recording. Also called an ET.

End Rate — The lowest rate at which a radio station is willing to sell commercial time.

Engineer — An individual licensed by the FCC to adjust transmitters and other broadcast equipment. Also, an individual who operates a board, i.e. a production engineer.

Equalization — The changing of the response of electronic equipment to accentuate certain frequencies more than others, especially in the broadcast or recording of various musical instruments.

ERP — Effective radiated power. A method of rating the power output of an FM radio station, taking antenna height and power of transmitter into account.

Ethnic Radio — A radio format directed at one or more racial, nationalistic, or cultural group.

Evergreen — A program segment which does not become outdated such as a historical piece.

Evening Time — Usually 7 P.M. to 12 Midnight on weekdays.

Exclusive Cume — The number of persons who stay tuned to a single station during a time period, such as a week or a month.

Fact Sheet — A compilation of information about the product or service of an advertiser from which commercial copy is prepared. Also called a spec sheet.

Fade — To increase or decrease gradually the volume of a sound to bring it in or take it out of the program, usually done electronically by means of a fader.

Fake It — Borrowed from the world of popular music, this expression in radio is an instruction to on-air talent to improvise, ad lib, and keep going although he has run out of prepared copy.

Fat — A fat program is one which runs overtime.

FCC or Federal Communications Commission — The Federal agency created in 1934 to regulate all interstate and foreign communication by wire and radio. Among other things, it has jurisdiction over the licensing and regulation of radio and television stations.

Feed — The delivery of a program by line or satellite.

Feedback — (1) The return of sound from a loudspeaker to the microphone in which it originated, creating a loud, shrill noise. (2) The expressed positive and negative criticism of a station by its audience.

Fidelity — The degree an electronic system is able to reproduce sound in close approximation to the original.

Fill — To add additional program content to use up excess time.

Filter — An electronic device used to screen out certain sound frequencies.

Fixed Position — A commercial presented at a specific, predetermined time during the broadcast day for which a premium is charged.

Flight — The time in which a cluster of commercials for one advertiser is carried without interruption over a station under a given contract.

Floater — On-air talent who seldom holds any job for very long.

Fluff — An announcer's mistake or goof.

FM or Frequency Modulation — A method of transmitting radio waves at frequencies from 88.1 MHz to 107.9 MHz.

Format — A radio station programming formula. The general arrangement of the programming presented by a station. Also, the identifiable type of programming of a station.

Four Book Average — The average ratings achieved by a station over four consecutive rating periods.

Freelancer — An independent individual (announcer, actor, producer, etc.) engaged to perform a specific function. Not a member of a radio station's staff.

Frequency — (1) The assigned channels at which AM and FM stations are located on dials; (2) Electrical term meaning cycles per second; (3) A rating term for the average number of times an individual is reached by an advertiser's spot over a specific period of time.

Frequency Discount — A discount given by a station or network to an advertiser who buys large amounts of commercial time.

Full-time Station — A radio station authorized to operate 24 hours a day whether or not it does so.

Gain — Volume or amplification of a tone or program.

Gross Cume — The total sum of the cume ratings for all of the stations in a plan of radio advertising.

Gross Impressions — The total number of times a commercial is heard during a given time period. Each listener is counted as one no matter how many times he hears the commercial.

Gross Rate — The cost of time on a radio station prior to the deduction of the advertising agency commission which is usually 15 percent.

Gross Rating Points or GRP — The sum total of radio ratings for each day-part and station, times the number of commercials of a given advertiser in each day-part on each station.

Ground Waves — Radio signals which flow from a transmitter and follow the contours of the earth.

Heads — Record, replay, and erase magnetic heads of tape recorders.

Hiatus — A break between flights by an advertiser when he schedules no commercial on a given station.

Hertz or Hz — One cycle per second.

Highs — High frequency sounds.

Hiss — High frequency noise, usually from a tape recording.

Hook — Any programming device (spoken, musical, sound effects, etc.) used to grab a listener's attention until he receives an entire message.

Horizontal Buy — A campaign or a flight of commercials placed throughout the broadcast week, often in an across-the-board program.

Hot Microphone — A live microphone capable of picking up sounds.

HUR — Homes using radio. A type of rating for radio in general, rather than for a specific program, station, or network.

Hypoing — The practice of inflating ratings by unusual and artificial means.

IBEW — A union of audio engineers; The International Brotherhood of Electrical Workers.

ID — A station identification giving its call letters and city of license. In advertising, a short announcement making mention of a sponsor.

Impedance — Microphones, speakers, and other electronic devices are rated numerically on their impedance factors. It is measured in ohms (a unit of resistance) and bears the symbol Z. Compatible impedances are necessary for electronic equipment to function properly.

Independent Station — A radio station that is not affiliated with a network.

Input — A program or sound source directed into a board or other equipment for distribution.

Insert — A program item placed in a slot within a longer program item.

Institutional Advertising — Copy designed to generate good will and enhance the image of the sponsor rather than sell its products or services directly.

Integrated Commercial — A single commercial promoting two or more separate products or services.

Interference — Static, conflicting signals, etc. which prevent proper reception of a signal.

Ionosphere — A layer of ionized particles 50 to 200 miles above the earth which, after sundown, reflects radio waves back to the earth. Also known as the Kennelly-Heaviside layer.

IPS — The speed or inches per second audio tape is recorded. The faster the speed, the higher the fidelity. Speeds range from 15/16ths to 30 inches per second.

Jingle — A musical signature or ID. Also, a musical commercial.

Kicker — A bright or cute news item, usually put at the end of a newscast.

Kill — To turn off a microphone. Cancel or stop a program dead.

Kilocycle or kC — A thousand cycles. A kilocycle per second equals a kilohertz.

Kilohertz or kHz — A thousand cycles per second. Also, the unit used to identify frequencies on the AM radio dial.

Kilowatt or kW — A unit of one thousand watts used to measure actual power output of AM stations and ERP of FM stations.

LBC — The last broadcast date for a flight.

Leader — Uncoded tape attached to the start of a tape reel for threading a tape recorder.

Lead-in — Program material used to set a scene or create a mood.

Leaking — Unwanted sound occurring through an input channel on a board, microphone, or other piece of equipment.

Level — The loudness or volume of sound as shown on a volume unit (VU) meter or other device.

License — An authorization issued by the FCC pertaining to a station or a related activity.

Licensee — The person or entity authorized by the FCC to own and operate a radio station.

Limiter — An electronic device which automatically prevents the volume of sound from exceeding a predetermined level.

Lines — Wire and telephone cables used to send program matter to and from radio stations. Long lines and extraterrestrial satellite transmissions are used in the transmitting and receiving of network programs.

Lip Microphone — A microphone held close to the mouth and used exclusively for speaking which excludes almost all background noises.

Live — A program, the majority of which is not recorded. Also, a live microphone is open, and live studio is one from which a broadcast is on the air or in the process of being recorded.

Live Copy — Advertising copy read live by an announcer.

Live Tag — A live insert added by an announcer within a recorded commercial.

Local Advertising — Advertising purchased by local business firms as distinguished from that purchased by regional and national advertisers.

Log — A daily record of a radio station's programming. Also, a technical register concerning various meter readings associated with transmitting equipment.

Logo — Short for logotype, a logo is used to establish a unique identity for a radio station or an advertiser's product or business through symbols and sounds.

Lows — Low or base sound frequencies.

LP — Long playing phonograph recordings played at 33 1/3 revolutions per minute.

Main Studio — The studio from which the majority of a station's local programming originates.

Make-good — A commercial run as a replacement for one not run when originally scheduled or for one in some other way not satisfactory to the advertiser.

Market — Generally, a radio station's sales area. Also, a specific geographically defined area of business activity.

Market Area — The population center served by a dominant radio signal.

Master — The original recording, i.e., the master tape, from which copies or dubs are made.

Master Control — The main control room used for producing programs and through which all programs must pass on the way to the station's transmitter.

MBS — Owner and operator of radio networks and stations; Mutual Broadcasting System.

MC — Master of ceremonies or host.

Media Mix — The use of two or more media for an advertising plan.

Media Plan — A statement for the use of funds to accomplish goals in an advertising campaign.

Megacycle or MC — A million cycles.

Megahertz or MHz — One million cycles per second. Also, the unit used to identify frequencies on the FM radio dial.

Metro Rating — A rating calculated for persons in a metropolitan area.

Metro Share — A radio station's share of the total listening in a metropolitan area by a specific targeted audience, stated in a percentage.

Metro Statistical Area or MSA — A geographical area designated by the Federal government and used by rating services.

Mix — The blending, balancing, and controlling of sound from various sources.

Mixer — A board or console used to mix sound.

Mobile Unit — A small broadcast studio built into a trailer, truck, or other vehicle, used to broadcast events on location.

Modulation — The process of varying the amplitude, frequency, or phase of a carrier or signal in radio and telephone.

Monaural — Sound from a single channel.

Monitor — A loudspeaker or a receiver in a control room for testing the audio quality of the program. Also, a device used to keep track of a radio station's programming by tape recording or written record.

MOR — Middle-of-the-road. Radio programming, music, and formats that are moderate and not extreme.

Morning Drive-time — The hours when workers are going to their places of employment, usually 6 A.M. to 10 A.M. in most markets.

Morning Man — On-air personality who works during morning drive-time.

Music Policy — The style of music featured by a station. Also, a written statement setting forth a station's method of selecting music.

NAB or National Association of Broadcasters — A trade association dedicated to the promotion of broadcasting and allied fields.

NABET — A union for broadcast technicians; National Association of Broadcast Engineers and Technicians.

Natural Sound — Real sound as opposed to sound effects.

NBC — Owner and operator of radio and television networks and stations; National Broadcasting Company.

Net Reach — The number of different individuals reached at least one time by a commercial during an advertising campaign. No individual is counted more than once.

Network — The originator of programs from a specific location which are broadcast at the same time on two or more affiliated stations. Program distribution is by telephone lines, microwave relays, and communications satellites.

Noise — All unwanted signals in a communications channel resulting in unplanned sound such as crosstalk, static, or other interference.

Nondirectional Microphone — A microphone which is equally sensitive in all directions.

Nondirectional Signal — A radio signal which is equally powerful in all directions. It is created by a transmitter which sends out a 360 degree signal.

NPR — A producer and distributor of fine art radio programming; National Public Radio.

NRBA or National Radio Broadcasters Association — A trade association dedicated to promotion of radio broadcasting and allied fields.

Off Mike — Sound originating away from the microphone creating a distant sound.

On Mike — Sound originating close to the microphone placing it in the audio foreground.

On The Nose — A program segment which starts or ends exactly on time.

One Time Only or OTO — Commercials ordered to run only once on a specific date.

O & O — Radio stations that are owned and operated by a network.

Open — The introductory announcement of a program.

Open Cold — To start a program with no introduction.

Open-end — Program formats which are perpetual. Only the on-air personalities change, but the format rolls on. Also, sports, conventions, and special events coverage that continues until the event ends.

Open Rate — The highest rate charged by a station for each day-part.

Out of Home — The audience listening to radio everywhere but at home.

Output — A program source leaving a board or console.

Overdubbing — A recording created on one or two channels by blending sound sources from a number of channels.

Package — A collection of recordings, commercials, or any items presented as a whole.

Pad — To fill with program matter until a certain time is reached.

Participating Program — A program with two or more advertisers, but with no overall sponsor.

Participations — Local broadcast announcements within programs.

Patch — To make an electrical connection for a broadcast, such as a telephone patch.

Payola — The unlawful undercover payment of money or other consideration to play certain records, to induce the use of certain programming, or to do some other commercial favor.

PBS — Owner and operator of nonprofit radio and television networks; Public Broadcasting Service.

Permittee — The person or firm authorized by the FCC to proceed under a construction permit.

Personality — A well known on-air talent who usually has his or her own show.

PI — Per inquiry advertising which is a system under which a station agrees to run spots and accept payment based on the results of the spots.

Pickup — To receive a radio transmission. Also, another term for phonograph stylus.

Piggyback — One commercial about two or more of advertisers' products.

Playback — To audition a recording.

Play List — A list specifying the recorded music to be played by on-air talent.

Plugola — Unlawful, unauthorized announcements about something in which the on-air talent secretly has an interest, which are not reported or logged as commercial matter.

Pot — The volume or gain control. Abbreviation for potentiometer.

Preempt — To replace regularly scheduled programming with a special presentation.

Prefade — To check a sound source for level and quality before it is faded up.

Preferred Position — A desirable position for commercials during the broadcast day for which an advertiser pays a premium.

Premium — An extra charge for a preferred commercial position.

Presence — The quality of certain sound that takes the listener into its environment.

Print Through — The transfer of an audio signal from one layer of tape to another, resulting in unwanted noise.

Printer — A teletype machine.

Producer — An individual who is in charge of the making of a program or commercial.

Product Protection — A guarantee as to the time that will separate commercials for products and services of competitors.

Program — A performance broadcast on radio. Also, a complete broadcast production or presentation.

Promo — An announcement which promotes any aspect of a radio station or its programming.

Proof of Performance — (1) Written evidence that the entire plant of a radio station meets FCC engineering specifications. (2) A sworn statement certifying that certain commercials or announcements were broadcast at certain times.

PSA or Public Service Announcement — A message broadcast by radio stations without charge on behalf of a nonprofit entity or governmental agency.

Psychographics — Data pertaining to the way the population of a given market divides into groups by behavioral patterns or reactions to emotional stimuli.

Public Domain — Creative materials not protected by common law or statutory copyright, available for use by anyone without payment of a royalty or fee.

Public Service Announcement — See PSA.

Punch — The reading of a line with intensity. A strong presentation.

PUR — Persons using radio. A type of rating for radio in general, rather than for a specific program, station, or network.

Quadrophonic Sound — Sound producing a three dimensional effect through four program channels.

RAB or Radio Advertising Bureau — A trade association, supported by the radio industry, designed to increase and improve the use of radio as an advertising medium.

RADAR Radio's All Dimension Audience Research — A semi-annual survey of national radio listening habits conducted for networks, prepared by Statistical Research, Inc.

Radio Spectrum — The entire number of frequencies available for radio utilization.

Rate — The cost per commercial announcement.

Rate Card — A concise printed statement which sets forth a radio station's current charges for commercials.

Rate Protection — The period of time in which a station charges an advertiser a constant rate although its published rates may be increased during that period.

Rating — An estimated measurement of the size of the total population of a given market and of the percentage of that population tuned to a specific station at a specific time.

Rating Service — A commercial research firm which estimates and measures local, regional, or national radio audiences.

Reach — The number of individuals that are estimated to be in the audience of a radio station at least once in a specified period of time. It may also be expressed as a percentage.

Rebate — An arrangement designed to give an advertiser a favorable rate through a reduction in the price or an increase in the number of units given to an advertiser.

Receiver — A device which detects radio signals and converts radio frequency waves into audio frequency waves that can be heard by the human ear.

Religion — A radio format.

Remote — A radio broadcast originating from a location other than a studio of the station.

Renewal — The extension of a radio advertising or program schedule on or before its expiration date.

Representative or Rep — The national sales representative of a radio station.

Resonance — Low register vibrations which impart fullness to a sound.

Reverberation — An electronic effect that stimulates an echo.

Ribbon Microphone — A bi-directional microphone which uses a narrow strip of foil supported within a strong magnetic field.

Ride Gain — The continual adjustment of pots to retain the highest transmission level possible.

ROS or Run of Schedule or Run of Station — The placement of the commercials of an advertiser throughout schedule at times selected exclusively by the station.

Rock — Rock'n roll music. A general category of radio formats.

Rotating Schedule — The placement of the commercials of an advertiser at various times within a day-part in order to reach the entire audience of that day-part.

RTNDA — Radio-Television News Directors Association.

Sandwich — A commercial composed of live copy inserted between a recorded opening and closing. Also called a donut or doughnut.

Saturation — The placement of the commercials of an advertiser in the schedule to reach the most listeners as quickly as possible, usually employed to announce a special retail sale or closeout.

Schedule — The times, days, and dates the announcements of an advertiser are to be run by a station.

Schedule Dates — The first and last dates of a flight or advertising campaign.

Schmaltz — A performance characterized by emotion and sentiment.

Script — The written text and instructions for performance and production of any broadcast segment.

Segue — The playing of two or more selections of music back to back without any interruption.

Sets In Use — The number of radio sets being used in a market during some period of time.

Sets In Use Rating — The percentage of all of the radio sets being used in a market during some period of time.

Share of Audience — The percentage of the aggregate radio audience in a

GLOSSARY   159

market that is in the audience of a given radio station, network, or program during some period of time.

Share of Market — The percentage or share of the total sales of a product or service accomplished by a firm.

Short Rate — The extra charge for commercial time assessed against an advertiser who uses fewer commercials than its original contract required, resulting in a higher rate per commercial.

Signal — A detectable electrical or electromagnetic impulse by which messages and information can be transmitted.

Signal Strength — The intensity of the signal of a station at a given distance from its transmitter.

Signal To Noise Ratio — The ratio of program sound to unwanted noise.

Sign Off — The time a station ends its broadcast day.

Sign On — The time a station starts its broadcast day.

Simulcast — A program broadcast by two or more stations in one market at the same time, usually on AM and FM or FM and television combinations.

Signature — An audio logo.

Sky Waves — Radio waves transmitted into the sky as opposed to ground-waves. They are lost during the daytime but reflect back to the earth off the ionosphere during the nighttime.

SMSA or Standard Metropolitan Statistical Area — An area composed of a major city and its suburban areas, determined by the Federal government, and used by various audience measurement services.

Sold Out — The lack of commercial availabilities when the commercial inventory of a station has all been sold.

Sound Effects or SFX — The sounds, other than words and music, used in radio programming of all types.

Sound Truck — A trailer or motor vehicle used for remote broadcasts.

Speaker — A loudspeaker.

Splicing — The joining of two pieces of audio tape with splicing tape.

Sponsor — An advertiser which pays the cost of a radio production in addition to the charges for commercial time.

Spot — An announcement on radio or television. Also, an advertisement for a product, service, or institution, also called a commercial.

Spot Announcement — A radio commercial not directly related to the program in which it is run.

Stand By — A warning used in a studio or on location that the microphones are about to go live for a broadcast or a recording.

Standard Broadcast Band — The AM frequencies from 535 kHz to 1605 kHz.

Station Break — An announcement of the call letters and city of license of a station, required by the FCC once each hour. Also called station identification.

Station Identification — See Station Break.

Stereophonic — Sound producing a three dimensional effect, usually over two or more channels.

Sting — The use of a piece of music for sharp emphasis.

Stock Music — The standard station library music, free of copyright, for use in commercials.

Stretch — A term used to slow down a program to fill to a specific time.

Stringer — A part-time newsperson who provides reports to radio stations and networks.

Strip — A program broadcast at the same time every day.

System Cue — A network identification used as a cue for affiliates to run local commercials in the time slots that follow.

Tag — An announcement added at the end of a recorded program or spot.

Take — The recording of a specific item or program, made at a single session. Also, a trial recording.

Take Down — The reception of programming from a communication satellite through a downlink.

Talent — A broadcast performer or entertainer. Also, a person with creative and/or artistic ability.

Talk — A radio format.

Talk Over — Talk by an airman over the first few bars of a musical selection.

TAP or Total Audience Plan — A package of commercials for use in those day-parts which give the advertiser's message the greatest reach.

Tape — The recording of program or commercial material on tape for broadcast or other uses.

Targeted Audience — The defined segment of the total audience of a market that a radio station or advertiser seeks to reach.

Tease — The introductory line of a program designed to provoke the interest of the audience and cause it to stay tuned for more.

Tens — Announcements which run 10 seconds each.

TF or Til Forbid; TN or Til Further Notice — A term meaning a schedule of commercials with no fixed termination date, designed to run until terminated by the advertiser or its agency.

Theme — A musical selection introducing a specific program.

Thirties — Announcements which run 30 seconds each.

Ticket — A license for a radio engineer or operator.

Tight — A program or unit with no dead air.

Time Period Rating — An audience measurement for a specific time rather than for a day-part.

Tone — A specific sound.

Total Survey Area or TSA — A geographical area, larger than a metro area, in which radio listening is measured.

Track — The sound of one channel on a tape.

Trade Out — The exchange of commercial time for merchandise and services.

Traffic — The department of a radio station that handles and schedules all announcements and provides product protection in accordance with station policy.

Transmit — The sending out of a signal either by radio waves or wire.

Transmitter — The device which converts sound into radio frequency waves and broadcasts those waves.

Transponder — A device capable of receiving, amplifying, and retransmitting a microwave signal. On a communications satellite, an incoming signal is received and automatically retransmitted by a transponder.

Trend — A comparison of a station's present book to previous estimates.

Unidirectional Microphone — A microphone which works in only one direction.

Uplink — An earth transmitting station, consisting of a dish type antenna or large parabolic reflector, capable of beaming a signal up to a communications satellite.

Useful Radio Spectrum — The total number of frequencies which may be used for the transmission of energy, communications, or signals by radio.

VU Meter — A meter which indicates volume units of sound passing through audio board or console.

Velocity Microphone — A ribbon microphone.

Watt — A unit of electrical power.

Wavelength — The distance between the beginning and ending of a single cycle of a radio wave.

Wire Copy — News, sports, weather, and information produced by the Associated Press, United Press International, and other news services and transmitted by teletype machines.

Wow — The distortion in recorded sound which is a slow rise and fall in pitch produced by variations in the speed of a turntable or tape player.

SELECTED BIBLIOGRAPHY

I. Books

Albert, Marv, and Hal Bock. *Yesss!: Marv Albert on Sportscasting.* New York: New American Library, 1979.

Associated Press, The. *Broadcast Style Book.* New York: AP.

Barber, W.L., and Robert Creamer. *Rhubarb in the Catbird Seat.* Garden City, New York: Doubleday, 1968.

Barnouw, Erik. *A History of Broadcasting in the United States to 1933.* New York: Oxford University Press, 1966.

— The Golden Web: *A History of Broadcasting in the United States, 1933-1935.* New York: Oxford University Press, 1968.

— *The Image Empire: A History of Broadcasting in the United States from 1953.* New York: Oxford University Press, 1970.

— *Tube of Plenty: The Evolution of American Television.* New York: Oxford University Press, 1975.

— *The Sponsor: Notes on an American Potentate.* New York: Oxford University Press, 1978.

Barton, Roger. *Advertising Agency Operations and Management.* New York: McGraw-Hill, 1955.

Barton, Roger, ed. *Handbook of Advertising Management.* New York: McGraw-Hill, 1970.

Bergreen, Laurence. *Look Now, Pay Later: The Rise of Network Broadcasting.* Garden City, New York: Doubleday, 1980.

Bliss, Edward J., ed. *In Search of Light; The Broadcasts of Edward R. Murrow, 1938-1961.* New York: Knopf, 1967.

Broadcasting Publications, Inc. *Broadcasting Yearbook.* Washington, D.C.: BPI.

Chester, Girand, Garnet R. Garrison, and Edgar E. Willis. *Television and Radio.* 4th ed. New York: Appleton-Century-Crofts, 1971.

Compaine, Benjamin M., ed. *Who Owns The Media?* New York: Harmony Books, 1979.

Cosell, Howard. *Cosell.* New York: Pocket Books, 1974.

Cronkite, Walter. *Challenges of Change.* Washington, D.C.: Public Affairs Press, 1971.

Crosby, John. *Out of the Blue.* New York: Simon and Schuster, 1952.

De Forest, Lee. *Father of Radio: The Autobiography of Lee De Forest.* Chicago: Wilcox and Fottett, 1950.

Denisoff, R. Serge. *Solid Gold: The Popular Record Industry.* New York: Transaction Books, 1976.

Dunning, John. *Tune in Yesterday: The Ultimate Encyclopedia of Old-Time Radio, 1925-1976.* Englewood Cliffs, New Jersey: Prentice-Hall, 1976.

Friendly, Fred W. *The Good Guys, the Bad Guys, and the First Amendment: Free Speech vs. Fairness in Broadcasting.* New York: Random House, 1976.

Gross, Ben. *I Looked and I Listened: Informal Recollections of Radio and TV.* New York: Random House, 1956.

Hale, Julian. *Radio Power: Propaganda and International Broadcasting.* Philadelphia: Temple University Press, 1975.

Hall, Claude, and Barbara Hall. *This Business of Radio Programming.* New York: Billboard, 1977.

Head, Sydney A. *Broadcasting in America.* 3d ed. (revised and enlarged). Boston: Houghton Mifflin, 1976.

Heighton, Elizabeth J., and Don R. Cunningham. *Advertising in the Broadcast Media.* Belmont, California: Wadsworth Publishing Company, Inc., 1976.

Hiebert, Ray Eldon, Donald E. Ungurait, and Thomas W. Bohn. *Mass Media II.* Longman, Inc., 1979.

Hilliard, Robert L. *Writing for Television and Radio.* New York: Hastings House, 1976.

Hilliard, Robert L., ed. *Radio Broadcasting.* New York: Hastings House, 1974.

Hoffer, Jay. *Organization & Operation of Broadcast Stations.* Blue Ridge Summit, Pennsylvania: Tab Books, 1971.

Hoffer, Jay and John McRae. *The Complete Broadcast Sales Guide For Stations, Reps & Ad Agencies.* Blue Ridge Summit, Pennsylvania: Tab Books, 1981.

Hyde, Stuart W. *Television and Radio Announcing.* Boston: Houghton Mifflin, 1971.

Johnson, Joseph S. and Kenneth K. Jones. *Modern Radio Station Practices.* Belmont, California: Wadsworth Publishing Company, Inc., 1978.

Kahu, Frank J., ed. *Documents of American Broadcasting.* New York: Appleton-Century-Crofts, 1968.

Kaltenborn, H.V. *Fifty Fabulous Years: 1900-1950.* New York: Putnam, 1950.

Kendrick, Alexander. *Prime Time: The Life of Edward R. Murrow.* Boston: Little, Brown, 1969.

King, Larry, and Emily Yoffe. *Larry King.* New York: Simon and Schuster, 1982.

Lerch, John H., ed. *Careers in Broadcasting.* New York: Appleton-Century-Crofts, 1962.

Lessing, Laurence. *Man of High Fidelity: Edward Howard Armstrong.* Philadelphia: Lippincott, 1956.

Lichty, Lawrence W., and Malachi C. Topping. *American Broadcasting: A Source Book on the History of Radio and Television.* New York: Hastings House, 1975.

Livingston, Mary, and Hilliard Marks. *Jack Benny: A Biography.* Garden City, New York: Doubleday, 1978.

Lyons, Eugene. *David Sarnoff: A Biography.* New York: Harper and Row, 1966.

Macdonald, Jack. *The Handbook of Radio Publicity and Promotion*. Blue Ridge Summit, Pennsylvania: Tab Books, 1970.

Miles, Donald. *Broadcast News Handbook*. Indianapolis: Howard W. Sams and Co., 1975.

Murphy, Jonne. *Handbook of Radio Advertising*. Radnor, Pennsylvania: Chilton Book Company, 1980.

National Association of Broadcasters. *Standard Definitions of Broadcast Research Terms*. January, 1967; rpt. Washington, D.C.: NAB, April, 1980.

Paley, William S. *As It Happened; A Memoir*. Garden City, New York: Doubleday, 1979.

Passman, Arnold. *The Deejays*. New York: Macmillan, 1971.

Quaal, Ward L. and Leo A. Martin. *Broadcast Management - Radio. Television*. 2d ed. (revised and enlarged). New York: Hastings House, 1978.

Robinson, Sol. *Broadcast Station Operating Guide*. Blue Ridge Summit, Pennsylvania: Tab Books, 1969.

Routt, Edd. *The Business of Radio Broadcasting*. Blue Ridge Summit, Pennsylvania: Tab Books, 1972.

Sarnoff, David, et al. *The Radio Industry: The Story of its Development*. Chicago: A.W. Shaw, 1928.

Schorr, Daniel. *Clearing the Air*. New York: Berkeley Publishing, 1978.

Swearer, Harvey F. and J. J. Carr. *Commercial FCC License Handbook*. 3d ed. Blue Ridge Summit, Pennsylvania: Tab Books, 1982.

United Press International. *Broadcast Style Book*. New York: UPI.

Wattenberg, Ben. *The Real America*. Garden City, New York: Doubleday, 1974.

Wells, Robert D., ed. *Life Style and Psychographics*, American Marketing Association, 1974.

White, Paul. *News on the Air*. New York: Harcourt, Brace, 1947.

II. *Periodicals*

Advertising Age, Chicago, weekly, 1930 ——

Annual Report of the Federal Radio Commission, annual, 1927-34.

Billboard, Cincinnati, originally monthly, now weekly, 1894 ——

Broadcasting, Washington, D.C., originally semimonthly now weekly, 1931 ——

FCC Reports, Washington, D.C., 1935 ——

Television/Radio Age, New York, biweekly, 1953 ——

Variety, New York, weekly 1905 ——

INDEX

ABC. *See* American Broadcasting Company

Account executives, 82, 86-88

Acting, 70-71

Adult Contemporary format, 52, 108

Adventure, crime, and mystery shows, 43

Advertisements, 81

Advertising agencies, 81-83, 86

Advertising copy, 88

Advertising, defined, 81-84

Aerials, 13

Affiliates, 42, 90, 110

Affiliation agreements, 90

Affirmative action programs, 4

Album Oriented Rock format (AOR), 53, 108

Alexanderson, Ernst, 10

Allen, Fred, 43

All News format, 53

All Talk/Information format, 53, 108

Alternating current, 12

AM. *See* Amplitude modulation

AM dial, 22

American Broadcasting Company (ABC), 16, 106, 108

American Telephone and Telegraph Company (AT&T), 105

Amos and Andy, 43

Amplitude modulation (AM)
characteristics, 24
frequencies, 22
stations, 11-19, 21-29, 32-33, 45-46, 91-101, 106, 144

Announcers, 71-80

Announcers, staff, 72

Antennas, 13, 25, 27-28

Antenna system, 100

AOR. *See* Album Oriented Rock

Arbitron Ratings Company (ARB), 48

Armstrong, Edwin H., 10, 24

AT&T. *See* American Telephone and Telegraph Company

Audience, measurement, 48-50
research, 48
size, 1, 7, 41-42, 68

Audio engineer, 103

Audion tube, 10

Barber, Red, 44

Beautiful Music format, 52, 108

Benny, Jack, 43

Bishop, Jerry, 115

Black format, 53

Blue Network, 105-106

Bob and Ray, 54

Branley, Edourd, 8

Brant Rock, Massachusetts, 10

Braun, Karl Ferdinand, 10

British Railway Act of 1887, 19

Broadcasting Yearbook, 52

Broadcast license, 1, 19-20, 32, 93-94

Broadcast roles, 70-80

Broadcast schedules, 56, 58

Broadcast specialists, 79-80

Bureau of Standards, 91

Business of broadcasting, 31-32, 81

Cain, Bob, 116-117
Call letters, 29
Canada, 29
Carrier waves, 11-13
Caruso, Enrico, 13
CBS. *See* Columbia Broadcasting System
C. E. Hooper Company, 48
Chanin, John G., 118-119
Chaotic use of frequencies, 91-93
Charlie Chan, 43
Chevrier, Don, 120
Chief engineers, 35, 101-103
Chief engineers' staffs, 103
Chief operators, 98
Chief operators, acting, 98
Children's programs, 43
Circulation, 48
City of license, 27
Classes of stations, 24-26
Classical format, 53, 76
Clearances, 111
Clear channels, 25
Columbia Broadcasting System (CBS), 16, 105
Columbia University, 10
Comedy, variety, and musical shows, 42-43
Commercial managers, 85
Commercial radio development, 13-20, 105-107
Commercials, forms, 88
  scheduling, 35, 66
  writing, 88
Commercial station defined, 33
Communications Act of 1934, 19, 24-25, 93
Communications Satellite Act of 1962, 107
Communications satellite systems, 107-109
COMSAT, 107
Congress, 18-19, 107
Coolidge, Calvin, 18
Copywriters, 88-89
Cornwall, England, 10
Corum, Bill, 44
Counterprogramming, 45
Country format, 52-53

Coverage, 48
Cox, James M., 16
Craig, Bob, 121
Crawford, Peter S., 122
Crosby, Bing, 42
Cumes, 50
Cumulative audience, 50
Cycles, 12

DeForest, Lee, 12-13
Demodulators, 108
Demographics, 48, 108-110
Diaries, Arbitron, 48-49
Dill-White Radio Act of 1927, 18
Direct current, 11-12
Directional signals, 27
Directors of engineering services, 101
Directors of technical operations, 101
Direct selling, 87
Disc jockeys (DJs), 2, 46, 55, 73-74
Distortion, 101
Downlinks, 108-109
Dual IDs, 27

Easy Aces, 43
Edison, Thomas A., 10
Education stations, 2, 23
Effective radiated power (ERP), 26
Electric currents, 11-12
Electricity, 11-12
Electric waves, 11-12
Electromagnetic field, 12
Electromagnetic spectrum, 21-22
Electromagnetic waves, 21-24
Electrons, 11
Engineering department, 98-103
Engineers, radio, 1-2, 9, 91-92, 94-103
Equal employment opportunities, 4
Equator, 107
ERP. *See* Effective radiated power
Ethnic format, 53, 108
Europe, 83
Experimental radio stations, 16, 91, 105

Faraday, Michael, 8
Farm programs, 44, 47

FCC. *See* Federal Communications Commission
Federal Communications Commission (FCC), creation, 19
    jurisdiction, 19-20
    regulation, 1, 4, 13, 18-20, 24-28, 31-33, 35, 46, 57, 59, 63, 93-102, 106-108, 111, 144
Federal Radio Commission (FRC), 18-19, 93
Fessenden, Reginald Aubrey, 10
Field strength, 98
First class tickets, 95
First Nighter, 42
FM. *See* Frequency modulation
FM dials, 23
Focus groups, 50
Footprints, 107
Formats, radio, 51-54
FRC. *See* Federal Radio Commission
Free enterprise system, 7
Frequency, alternation, 12
Frequency check, monthly, 100-101
Frequency modulation (FM)
    characteristics, 24
    frequencies, 23
    stations, 11-19, 21-29, 32-33, 45-46, 91-101, 106, 108, 144

Gangbusters, 43
General managers, 32-36, 85, 102
General radiotelephone operator license, 97
General sales managers, 35, 85-86
Geosynchronous orbit, 107
GHz. *See* Gigahertz
Gigahertz (GHz), 12
Gigawatt (GW), 12
Goldbergs, The, 43
Golden Age of Radio, 41-45, 90, 105
Goodman, Dona S., 123-124
Green Hornet, The, 43
Groundwaves, 24
Group owned stations, 32, 89
GW. *See* Gigawatt

Harding, Warren G., 16

Hertz (Hz), 8, 12
Hertz, Heinrich Rudolph, 8, 10
Hooper, C. E., 48
Hope, Bob, 42
Hopper, Hedda, 43
Hosts, music, 73-76
Households, 68
Housewive's hour, 44
Human hearing, 23
Husing, Ted, 44
Hz. *See* Hertz

Images, 21, 64
Impact of radio, 1, 7-8, 83-84
Imus, Don, 125
Independent stations, 42, 46
Inspection and maintenance log, weekly, 100
International agreements, 29, 91
Interstate Commerce Act of 1887, 19
Ionosphere, 24

Jack Armstrong, The All American Boy, 43
Jackson Heights, 83
Jazz format, 29, 76

KABL, 29
Kaiton, Chuck, 126-127
Kaltenborn, H. V., 44
KDKA, 16, 29
Kennelly-Heaviside layer, 24
KFOG, 29
KHz. *See* Kilohertz
Kilohertz (kHz), 12
Kilowatt (kW), 12
KJAZ, 29
KJZZ, 29
KMPC, 29
KNX, 29
KOOL, 29
KYW, 29
KW. *See* Kilowatt

Landlines and charges, 16, 107, 112
Let's Pretend, 43
Libel, 7
Licensed operators, 93-97

Licensing of stations, 1-2, 18-20, 93-94, 106
  termination, 32
Light, speed of, 23
Line-of-sight, 24
Local loops, 108
Local sales, 84-85
Lone Ranger, The, 43
Lux Radio Theater, 42

Mack, Nila, 43
Mail from listeners, 70
Ma Perkins, 43
Marconi, Guglielmo, 8, 10
Maxwell, James Clerk, 8
MBS. *See* Mutual Broadcasting System
McBride, Mary Margaret, 44
McCarthy, Donna Rustigan, 128
McLannahan, Byron N., 129-130
McNamee, Graham, 44
Media, 81-83
Megahertz (MHz), 12
Megawatt (MW), 12
Mellow Rock formal, 53
Mercury Theater, The, 42
Metropolitan Opera, 105
Mexico, 29
MHz. *See* Megahertz
Microphones, 11
Microwave links, 100, 108
Mississippi, 29
Missouri, 105
Mixed media campaign, 82
Modulation, 23
Morning man, 74
Morse Code, 10
Multiple network ownership, 16, 105-106
Murrow, Edward R., 44
Music, 52, 60-61
Music director, 60-61
Mutual Broadcasting System (MBS), 16, 106
MW. *See* Megawatt

National Broadcasting Company (NBC), 12, 16, 105-106, 108
National Public Radio (NPR), 110
National radio conferences, 18-19

National sales, 85, 89-90
National sales directors, 85
National sales representatives, 85, 89-90
NBC. *See* National Broadcasting Company
Network satellite configuration, 107-109
Networks, 16, 18, 41-45, 105-112
  administration and management, 110-112
  executives, 111
  formats, 108, 110
  regulation, 111
  sales, 85
  staff, 90
  targeted audiences, 108-110
New Music format, 53
News and Information Service, 108
News and public affairs, 44
Newscasters, 76-77
News, defined, 62
News directors, 61-62
New York Giants, 16
New York, New York, 16, 105
New York Yankees, 16
Nobel Prize, 10
Noncommercial radio, 1, 110
Nondirectional signals, 27
Nostalgia format, 53
NPR. *See* National Public Radio

Office manager, 35
Orbits, 107
Our Gal Sunday, 43

Parker, Charlie, 131-132
Parsons, Luella, 43
Payola, 61
Pell, Ron, 133-134
Perry, Jim, 134-135
Petry, Edward, 89
Pilot of the Airwaves, 67
Plugola, 61
Prerogatives of owners, 57
Primary signals, 24
Production directors, 63-64
Professions of radio, 1
Program directors, 34, 57-66, 69
Program elements, 58

Program formats, 52-54, 56
Programming objectives, 57
Programming policy books, 58
Program patterns, 51-52, 56
Program syndicators, 56
Promotion, audience, 64-65
   sales, 84-88
Promotion directors, 64-65
Proof of performance report,
   annual, 101
"Public interest, convenience and
   necessity," 32, 93
Public radio stations, 1, 55

Queensboro Corporation, The, 83
Quiz, game, and talk shows, 43-44
Quiz Kids, The, 43

Radio Act of 1912, 18
Radio Corporation of America
   (RCA), 13, 16, 83
Radio drama, 42
Radio industry, 1, 7
Radio signals, 11, 13, 27
Radio spectrum, 19, 21-23, 25, 93
Radio station operator licensees,
   1-2, 18-20, 93-94, 106
Radio station operators, 93-97
Radiotelephone operator licenses,
   94-97
Radio waves, 11, 13, 27
Rasmussen, William F., 136
Rating, 50
Ratings, 28-29, 34, 48-50, 57
Ratings book, 48
RCA. *See* Radio Corporation of
   America
Receivers, 7, 13
Red Network, 105
Religion format, 54
Restricted radiotelephone operator
   license, 94-97
Robinson, Dick, 137
Rogers, Will, 105
Rolling Stones, 58
Romance of Helen Trent, The, 43
Roosevelt, Franklin D., 19

St. John's, New Foundland, 10
Sales department staff, 84-89

Sales director, 85
Salespersons, 86-88
Sarnoff, David, 13, 83
Schneider, Paula E., 138-139
Secondary signals, 24
Second class radiotelephone
   license, 97
Senate, 19
Shakespeare, William, 30
Share of audience, 50
Simulcasting, 46
Sitcoms. *See* Situation comedies
Situation comedies (Sitcoms), 43
Skip, 24
Skywaves, 24
Slander, 7
Slogans, 28-30
Soap operas (Soaps), 43
Soaps. *See* Soap operas
Sound, 23-24
Sound effects, 63-64
Spanish format, 53
Spitzer, Elton L., 140-141
Splatter, 24
Sportscasters, 63, 77, 79
Sports directors, 62
Sports, play-by-play, 63, 77
Sports programming, 44, 62-63,
   77-79, 108
Spot sales. *See* National sales
S.S. Republic, 13
S.S. Titanic, 13
Standard band, 22
Station identification, 26-27
Station organizational charts,
   38-40
Station sound, 51
Stern, Bill, 44
Studio equipment, 100
Superheterodyne circuit, 10
Superman, 43
Suspense, 43
Symbols, 28-30

Take It Or Leave It (The $64 Ques-
tion), 43
Talk show hosts, 79
Targeted audiences, 46-50, 56
Targeted markets, 48

Television's rise, 45, 106
Test equipment, 100
Thomas, Lowell, 44
Tower light inspection reports, quarterly, 100
Traffic managers and staffs, 35, 66
Transmitter engineers, 103
Transmitter operating logs, 100
Transmitting systems, 100
Transponders, 107
Trends, 50
Triode tube, 10
Truth or Consequences, 43
Two-way radio systems, 100

United States, 108
University of Wisconsin, 16
Uplinks, 107, 109

Vacuum tubes, 10
Vibrations, 11-13, 23-24

WABC, 16, 29
WACO, 29
Waldorf Astoria Hotel, 105
WARE, 29

Wavelengths, 12
WBZ, 16, 29
WCBS, 29
WEAF, 83
WGN, 29
WGY, 16
Wheeler, Walt, 142-143
WILD, 29
WIND, 29
Wireless, 10
Wireless Ship Act of 1910, 18
WJZ, 16
WKSS, 29
WMGK, 29
WNBC, 29
WNEW, 29
WOR, 29
Working conditions, 4
World War I, 10
World War II, 44
World's first radio program, 10
WQXR, 29
Writing, 2, 88-89
WWJ, 16

About The Author

Radio has always been an important part of Dan Blume's life. An announcement of his birth was broadcast by WTIC, Hartford, Connecticut, his home town, during a program featuring a string ensemble directed by his father. He made his first on-air appearance on WTHT, Hartford, [now WINF, Manchester] as a member of a fifth grade discussion group. While an undergraduate at the University of Connecticut, Dan took his first regular shift in radio on WHUS, Storrs, also known as The Husky Network. In the late 50's, he worked as an on-air performer and writer for radio stations and networks in the Washington, D.C. area. He served as the host of Southern New England's first jazz show in FM stereo on WBMI (FM), Hartford-Meriden, [now WKSS (FM)] in the mid 60's. He recently wrote and served as the host of a show called *Sports, The Legal View*, heard coast-to-coast on the Enterprise Radio Network.

A graduate of UConn and Georgetown University Law Center, Dan is presently a Hartford lawyer and a member of the FCC Bar Association. He is also associated with a group that owns five radio stations in New York.

Dan resides in West Hartford, Connecticut, with his wife Joanne, son Jared, and daughter Meredith.

Notes

Notes